A PARENT'S GUIDE TO EARLY COMMUNICATION

JUMP-START YOUR CHILD'S INTERACTION AND LANGUAGE SKILLS TOWARDS FIRST WORDS AND PHRASES

7 POWERFUL STRATEGIES WITH TRANSFORMATIVE VIDEO EXERCISES

CAROLYN J. WEBB

First published by DIY Speech Therapy 2023

First edition

Disclaimer

Parents and caregivers are strongly advised to seek the guidance of a professional as early as possible if there are any concerns about a child's speech, language or communication skills. This book is not intended to replace therapy or the direct support of a speech and language pathologist or therapist. Its purpose is to educate parents and caregivers as they support their child. Results are not guaranteed. A child's progress in communication will depend on many factors. This book can be a useful tool to help support parents and caregivers while their child is attending a speech and language therapist.

TABLE OF CONTENTS

Do you want to learn about the one thing you can do now to best promote communication between you and your child?

Grab your Free Tip Sheet Here!

https://bit.ly/41lAEAT

ABOUT THE AUTHOR

Carolyn has over 30 years of experience as a Speech and Language Therapist in Ireland and is committed to helping parents support their children's communication development. She now works independently with parents and caregivers from all over the world, helping them find fun, manageable ways to encourage and support their children's communication development. She has previously worked in various settings, including Community Health, Preschool Units, Primary School Units, Child and Adolescent Mental Health Multidisciplinary Teams and draws on all her extensive practical experience to guide and coach parents and caregivers, for the most effective outcomes in the shortest amount of time.

This book shares strategies that Carolyn regularly uses to coach parents as their young children start learning to communicate. She has found these strategies to be the most effective way to help parents connect with their children. This is important because connection promotes communication. She has written this book to share the 'how to', with broken-down easy steps and transformative video exercises to try at home. The hope is that parents and caregivers will find this book's easy and often impactful communication strategies helpful and make the most difference..

***Carolyn also offers online coaching consultation sessions to parents worldwide. If you would like to book a free 15 minute call with Carolyn to find out more about this, please email* info@diyspeechtherapy.com.**

"Special thanks to my own family and to all the wonderful families, friends and colleagues I have had the pleasure of crossing paths with. Each one of you has contributed to this book in some way!"

Carolyn

FOREWORD

HELLO!

First of all, thank you for putting your trust in this book. Let me tell you a little about myself so you understand the purpose of what we are trying to do. It has been a joyful and occasionally challenging experience to be a mom of a now teenage boy. I am also a mom to two cats, Gadget and Widget (alias 'Missy Moo'), who entertain me daily. One has recently learned to use large buttons to ask for his preferred food for the day. When he chooses and presses a button from the 'menu' with his paw, it speaks the name of his desired food. Yes, this is what happens when you have a Speech Therapist for a human mom!

When I approach a problem, I think visually. I have to fully examine something in detail to understand it inside and out, break it down, and explain it well. I have also spent many years working with and listening to parents with a common goal: supporting their children to grow and develop to the best of their ability.

Many parents have told me over the years that it is all just so complicated! There are many steps, things to do, varying approaches, theories, advice, and complex textbooks outlining ways to help children develop their communication skills. Parents often feel overwhelmed and don't know where to begin.

They tell me they feel under pressure because there is a 'window of opportunity' to get in and help children progress. Often, they have to wait a very long time to see a professional. And when they are finally offered an appointment, they are often given either spoken or written information in complicated reports or advice sheets and then have to go back on a waiting list again to access therapy sessions. Parents tell me that the advice, reports, summary sheets, and references help them understand what to do, but they are still unsure if they are carrying out the guidance correctly.

When they are eventually offered therapy sessions, it's great! But parents tell me they rely on continually attending the therapy for it to work. They say that because the sessions may be few and far between, there often isn't enough time to learn what to do properly. So parents copy what they see during the sessions and do bits and pieces at home, hoping on a wing and a prayer that they are doing the right thing. Then, the set number of therapy sessions ends. While waiting to be called back in, parents can feel lost at sea again without the support of ongoing guidance.

I see how frustrating it can be for parents who often have to wait far too long to access therapy when I know from my work that there are small things anyone can do from very early on that can help children connect, interact more, and will ultimately lay down the foundations for communication.

This is what has motivated me to write this book. It is based entirely on my own experience over many years of working in this field. Although all these strategies are well recognized and evidence-based, you will find few outside references here because everything you will read is about how I do therapy in a granular detailed way, straight from the horse's mouth.

My goal was to demystify valuable speech therapy techniques and make them easily accessible so you can start making a difference right now. So, I needed to find a way to translate the advice (often given in bullet points) into real examples and experiences to create lasting change. I needed to find a way to clearly outline some key tips that no one has really been able to explain properly before, and I also needed to provide a framework so that you are not just reading about it but also trying it out for yourself – with helpful pointers along the way. So read on if this feels like a good fit for you.

WHY ME?

So you have identified that your child is not progressing in their language skills, interacting or communicating at the rate you thought they would. You might prefer someone else to identify the problem, come up with a plan, and for that person to do all the necessary therapy to fix it. And yes, wouldn't this be great! We'd all love a magic wand to zap around and fix all the laundry or that unreachable lightbulb. If only we could wiggle our noses and make things appear or disappear, just like that show about a genie from the 1960's (I'm showing my age now!).

But remember that you are your child's first playmate. You are with them most of the time. As 'Mom' or 'Dad', you literally *are* their world. They are more likely to connect with you than someone new who comes along and tries to intervene in what they are doing. Also, when a therapist works with your child for one hour a week, you still have to do the strategies during the days in between the sessions! One hour a week won't achieve much on its own. It is the regularity of using the tools little by little, day by day, to deepen the connection between you and your child that will have the most impact on their ability to communicate with you.

If you are reading this book, it may be because you already think your child has some communication needs. That is a good enough reason to start using strategies now. But these strategies are not just for children with identified communication needs. All children benefit and enjoy deeper connections with their parents, along with longer-lasting 'to-and-fro' interactions. So, your efforts won't be wasted even if you are unsure that your child is experiencing language, interaction, or communication challenges. You will be helping promote more opportunities for your child to reach their next milestone.

I want you to imagine yourself in two alternative work situations: in one scenario, your boss is kind but remote and 'lets you get on with it'.

In the other scenario, your boss is equally kind but comes over to chat with you regularly with a smile on their face. Your boss doesn't talk about work or deadlines. Instead, your boss listens to how your day is going, to your daily challenges, and enjoys hearing about your family and your world.

Now, in which scenario would you be more likely to approach your boss for an unsolicited chat? Yes, the scenario where your boss makes an effort and connects with you! Where your boss takes the time to listen about your trip to the mountains at the weekend or how your child has a bug and kept you up all night. The things that are important to *you*.

We have to do these same things to entice our children to want to connect with us more. And we know that connection leads to communication.

BUT I'M ALREADY DOING IT!

Yes, you are! You are doing lots already. But we can always do more of it, and in such a way that targets specific aspects of communication that can make a big difference down the line. The goal is for your child to connect with you even more, which can help them get ready to learn new things, including communication.

This book is not intended to change everything you are doing. Think of it more as tweaking what you are already doing in your daily activities and the fun things you already do together to maximize the opportunities for communication during those times.

Quality is always better than quantity: A few short minutes of valuable interaction and connection with your child is enough. Don't try to over-achieve. Young children have short attention spans anyway and may flit from one thing to the next, just like a butterfly. We can adapt to their ways and go with the flow alongside them, and they will still benefit! We don't need to sit down and 'do work' with our children. Natural fun play leads to genuine communication, just like the scenario with your boss.

Approach each strategy with an open mind. As parents, we may develop certain ways we like to do things. Sometimes, those ways work well. But sometimes we may not realize when they are not working, or when there is another way that would work better. It can be hard to change or break these little habits we pick up. Taking on new ways of doing things requires humility and flexibility, as we must reflect and acknowledge when things might not work at their best. That's okay! This is what therapists have to do all the time. We try, we fail, we figure it out and try again. There are only positive things to be gained from this process. Heck, I'm still learning, and I've been doing this since 1986!

We must also remember that each child is unique, with different likes and dislikes. Children may have different ability levels, but each child is at the right level for them right now. I try to give a range of examples from experiences in clinical practice to make the strategies real and accessible. The examples given may not exactly reflect how your child is, but if you notice a similarity, try to find a way to adapt the main gist of each strategy to you and your child. Be flexible! You can't go wrong as long as your child is having fun.

IMPORTANT: Bear in mind also that your child may have sensitivities unique to them: for example one child may love tickles, another may hate them. ***Never*** persist with any of the suggestions or examples given if you notice your child has any kind of dislike or aversion to it. Find their own likes and adapt the examples and suggestions to them.

As you try each strategy out, you'll feel more and more empowered and confident in doing little things to make a difference in your child's communication skills. Remember: you are important. Every small tweak you make can help your child progress in little ways. All these little wins build up over time.

Communication and Language: What's the Difference?

As therapists, we use these and other terms regularly. But what do each of these words actually mean? Here is a list of some of the words you'll find in this book:

Engagement refers to when your child notices you and starts to pay attention. They may even interact with you and stay engaged with you for longer and longer.

Interaction is a connection or exchange between two people, often without words. For example, when you throw a ball back and forth to each other, or play a fun tickle game and your child wriggles to ask for more, or when you hand things to your child and they look towards you or reach out to look for another – these are all examples of interaction.

Vocalization refers to any sound your child makes that is not a word. For example, any little sighs and sounds involving the voice, even the grumbling noises your child makes when they are not too happy!

Chatter is a term used in this book to refer to long strings of vocalizations or babble. It might sound like a conversation, but there are few or no understandable words. If your child uses chatter, we will talk about how to support them later during Strategy 4: Respond with Enthusiasm.

Communication is the broad umbrella term for anything that sends a message to anyone, either with words or without words, like in the examples we just mentioned. Communication can happen by using body language and facial expressions, words, hand signs, pictures, written text, or through a device with icons or images to interact and communicate something to someone.

AAC refers to any form of aided communication using hand signs, pictures, or a device like a tablet with special software. AAC stands for 'Augmentative and Alternative Communication'.

Language refers to any system of symbols that communicates something to someone else. This could be through spoken words, written words, hand signs, pictures, the written word or an AAC device. In this book, the term 'language' will refer to spoken language, but you can apply all the same principles to whatever system your child uses or will be using in the future.

Non-speaking is used in this book to refer to children who are not yet using understandable words. This does not mean that they don't have any internal language. We all have language inside, but non-speaking children do not yet outwardly show signs of this.

Minimally speaking refers to children who may be able to use some words but may not yet use them regularly to communicate in everyday situations.

Modeling refers to what we say in such a way that a child can manage to understand our message. It can also refer to providing a good example of what a child could say when they are ready. This very much depends on where a child is at in their communication development. We will talk about modeling during Strategy 4: Respond with Enthusiasm.

Self-Agency in this book refers to the ability to act as an agent for oneself: to make choices and decisions about one's needs or wants and express these to others.

Expression is a term used to refer to *how* a child expresses their wants and needs or shares information with others.

Understanding refers to a child's ability to understand what is communicated to them.

Try to familiarise yourself with these terms. It will make it easier for you when we talk about the strategies later on. You can also bookmark this page to check back if needed.

I WANT MY CHILD TO TALK

When their child is non-speaking or minimally speaking, parents often say to me, 'I want my child to talk.'. But we learn to *interact* first, long before we use words. Interaction mimics the idea of a 'to and fro' in conversation, back and forth, with each person doing something in turns. And this all starts without any words at all.

So you can see that if your child is not yet engaging in a 'to and fro' interaction without words, then trying to teach them to say words is a bit like asking them to run before they can walk. It doesn't mean they won't get there, but we must focus on building the foundations first.

Suppose your child is not yet interacting in many different ways *without* words, in many different situations, or in a back-and-forth 'to-and-fro' way. If this is the case, then that will be what you can focus on first - interaction. We cannot skip this step or go straight to focusing on words. But the good news is that there are lots of simple things we can do right away to help them on their journey towards words. We can use strategies to help children develop more ways to communicate without words and to engage in fun for longer, to-and-fro interactions with you.

Even children who are already using words can benefit from focusing on interaction because interaction is such an essential component of how we communicate with each other. For example, when we have conversations with our friends, it's not just about the information they share with us. What we really want is to connect and enjoy our time together, and feel like the conversation is flowing easily back and forth.

Maybe your child readily interacts with you regularly throughout the day. In this case, we focus on *why* they communicate with you. Some children will only really communicate when they need or want something; for example, by coming over to you, leading you by the hand, reaching for what they want, or handing you something.

Another reason your child might send you a message might be to make it clear they don't want or like something by using sounds of frustration, pushing away your hand, or moving themselves away.

For example, when you offer them the wrong snack or toy, or if you go to wipe their mouth with a cold, wet cloth!

If your child is at this step of showing what they want and don't want, then we are looking for them to ask for your help in new situations and in new ways.

For example, suppose your child communicates by handing you the remote when they want to watch TV. I'm using this particular example because for some children I work with, this is when they have the most motivation to communicate. In this case, we might focus on encouraging them to hand you other things too. Or we could watch closely for other ways they might ask you to watch TV and respond to those attempts too: They could do this by leading you by the hand towards the TV or making sounds while near the TV. We are also looking to increase the frequency of their attempts at communicating with you. The goal is to empower your child so they can make more requests in their own way, not to teach them something *we* want them to do – more on this later!

JOINT ATTENTION

Does your child mainly communicate to show what they want or don't want without words? Or does your child also communicate for another reason: to *share* something fun with you – without asking for you to do anything specific?

We call this *joint attention*: the ability to share focus on something together with someone else where we know the other person is also looking and paying attention with us.

When joint attention happens, there is an unspoken understanding that both of you are looking at or paying attention to the same thing.

We see this if your child brings something to you or lifts something up to show it to you just for fun – not because they need your help, not for you to fix it or do anything about it. They show it to you because it's fun, intriguing, or it's something they like. They want you to see the fun or intriguing thing too so you can share the fun together.

Children show that they have developed good joint attention skills when they can show you or point to things that excite them across various situations, like showing you their favorite picture in a book, pointing to things of interest out the window or in the park. There will also be some signs that they are waiting for you to look too. Some children may point to something and look back at you to check that you are also looking. But even without making eye contact, your child can still share joint attention with you. The key point is that they are not *asking* for anything; they are just *sharing* something with you for fun and want you to notice too.

There are two main ways to focus on joint attention:

Joint Attention Step 1

Step 1 is where your child becomes aware when you point to something and follows where you are indicating by looking towards where you are pointing. This is usually easiest in the space immediately in front of them, where they are already looking. For example, does your child glance over when you point to something on the page of a book or when playing with some objects or toys right in front of them, like blocks or a train set? If you notice something intriguing, point to it and say, 'Look at this! Wow!'. Does your child follow and glance towards what you are showing them?

Then, as your child understands the concept of your pointing, you can begin to point or draw your child's attention to things that are further away. Can they follow when you point to something across the room? Will they go towards the area? Or will they look when you point to something outside the window? Or something a little further away when on a walk? Or a plane in the sky?

When your child is ready and showing interest in your pointing, then commenting and pointing to things your child seems interested in at various times of the day is a great way to help them move forward. You can give them many opportunities to understand the power of pointing to communicate something. You are modeling some great ways for them to do it later when ready. It also helps them to learn what your words mean when you point and say something about it (Look! it's all wet / it's so big! / they're falling down!'!). Don't worry if your child isn't following your point yet. You can continue offering opportunities here and there throughout the day by pointing out intriguing things, naturally. In time, they will start to notice.

When your child has developed the ability to follow your point in many of these situations, then they are likely ready for Step 2.

Joint Attention Step 2

Step 2 is where your child starts to hold something up or point to things to show you. You cannot force this step; They will reach Step 2 and begin to show you things when ready. Your role is purely to model joint attention by pointing, showing and commenting for your child on the things they find intriguing (Step 1).

I would not recommend using 'hand over hand' techniques to 'teach' pointing as this may result in a learned response. Learned responses are not natural. Plus, we want to respect a child's bodily autonomy wherever possible, and taking their hand if they haven't asked for it can take away their sense of control over their own body.

When they are ready, some children may start trying to point to things by using their whole hand instead of using a pointing finger - A great first step. Or they might point without a clear plan of what they are pointing to, for example, randomly 'pointing' repeatedly on a page in a book. This is a great start and to be encouraged! You can respond when they make these attempts by smiling, nodding, and commenting conversationally about what you think they might be trying to show you. 'Yes! I see it too!' 'That's a...'.

If your child is already starting to use pointing, it is helpful to look at *why* they are pointing. Is it because they like the feel of the pointing? Are they pointing and waiting for you to do or say something? Both are good! It's just good to know where they are at so that you know how you can connect with your child at that moment. If they like the feel of it, then join in, feel it too, comment and point! If they are pointing and waiting for you to do or say something, then you can Respond with Enthusiasm (Strategy 4).

EYE CONTACT

Eye contact is not something I recommend focusing on anymore: I no longer choose eye contact as a goal for a child to request something from me. All this does is train a child to do something that may not come naturally to them or urges them to do it when they are not ready. Certain children may even feel uncomfortable looking directly at others' faces or eyes, so why put them through that? I know it has been such a staple for therapists in the past to focus on increasing eye contact, but the reality is that a child will naturally make eye contact if and when they are ready and able to. There are other things we can do that will be more helpful for promoting interaction and communication instead. Again, more on this later!

Some children have specific difficulty shifting their attention – this means that when they look down at whatever they are focusing on, it can be really challenging for them to disengage their attention from what they are doing and look up at a person's face. Usually, the person is towering above them anyway – when you think about it, our eye level as adults will usually be higher than a child's, even when both are sitting! We will address some things we can do about this in our strategies.

Other children flit quickly from one activity to the next, so it can be hard to keep up: as soon as you sit with them and start to get involved, they drop what they are doing and move on to something else. So you might feel like you don't get a chance to spend any quality time on anything in particular. Don't worry if this is the case. Your child will still benefit from your support if you follow the strategies in this book. Attention skills develop over time. Eventually, you may notice your child sticking with one activity a little longer and tuning into you when they are ready. You can help them stay engaged with you by focusing on movement games that they really enjoy rather than expecting them to remain involved with you *and* a toy at the same time.

Right! We have covered some useful background information, and now it's time to get started with our very first strategy. Read each strategy all the way through first to get a feel for what we are trying to achieve. Then read back over it again and focus on the parts that you feel are relevant to you and your child. Make notes as you go or underline the parts you connect with. You can repeat this process for each strategy. There will be exercises and challenges to do each step of the way. Remember to abandon any activity or strategy if your child is not in the mood or if they actively dislike it. We are not here to make anyone feel uncomfortable.

DO NOT SKIP THE CHALLENGES! They are there to make sure that you put the strategies into practice. If you skip the challenges, the information you are learning may not translate into real change for you or your child. We want to practice those tweaks, little by little, starting right away so that you and your child can reap benefits as soon as possible! You may not fully realize why we need to pay so much attention to what seems like simple things - please trust the process and go with it!

Please remember our goal is *always* to create or follow as much joy as possible. It is not helpful to 'sit down and do work' for extended periods as your child likely won't enjoy it. It is more effective if you include strategies during your fun natural interactions in short bursts as the occasions arise spontaneously throughout the day.

There are no 'have to's' when it comes to how long to spend using your strategies. The length of time a child will be open to connecting varies from individual to individual, with their mood, health, hunger/tiredness levels, and so on. Plus, the goal of practicing the strategies is more about *you* than your child. I would recommend practicing your strategies for several minutes a day - when you and your child are both in the mood. But adapt this depending on your schedule and your child's ability and mood.

You are aiming to become the best possible communication partner for your child.

This takes practice over time. It is enough to practice your strategies here and there a few times a day - even for 30 seconds at a time - if that is all you or your child can manage. If your child shows you they are no longer interested, drop it and wait for the next time they are receptive. One day, you may find lots of opportunities to build connection. On other days, you may simply need to focus on getting through that day, and that's okay!

If you can use your strategies in a planned way more than once a day, then great! The ideal goal of regular practice is for the strategies to become so natural for *you* that you use them automatically as part of your everyday interactions with your child without thinking twice about it. It is the cumulative effect that will make the difference, bit by bit, over time.

If you have the time available and if your child is having fun, I would recommend actively engaging in strategies in a planned way for a few minutes at a time and then stopping so your child can get back to doing what they like or playing in their own space or in their own way again. That way, you will avoid overwhelming either yourself or your child. Setting yourself a timer for 3 to 5 minutes can be very effective so that you have a clear focus for those few minutes.

If your child seeks you out and you can give them the time, then you could increase the amount of time you spend practicing the strategies, but this is not necessary. A few minutes a day is enough! Even if you or your child has an 'off' day, that's okay! Don't worry about the strategies when this happens. Focus on keeping yourself and your child regulated and calm until things are better and you are both more in the mood to engage. You can always try again tomorrow. Keep showing up and trying a little each day.

Remember too that communication is a broad umbrella term: If your child is already using signs, pictures, or an AAC device to communicate, or if one of these systems has been recommended, then the strategies in this book still apply. You can ask your therapist to show you how to adapt your child's AAC device or communication system to include relevant sound effects, words, and phrases that reflect your child's interests and joy based on what you learn in this book. As a parent, *you* are in the best position to identify some of these key things to communicate about with your child.

Time to get started!

INTRODUCTION

Knowing where to start can be challenging when you realize your child is not yet talking. You may be a parent of a young child who only connects with you when they want something, need your help, or to let you know they don't like something. Perhaps your child has lots of fun with you during fun physical play but is not using language effectively to communicate with you in a back-and-forth way in everyday situations. If this sounds familiar, then I'm so glad you have stumbled upon this book.

Poured into this is a distillation of everything I have learned over the years: all the study, clinical practice, and the many courses, continuous professional development and learning. All this information has been streamlined into the core strategies that I consider to be the best ones to achieve the most results in the shortest amount of time. I have also included the random things I have tried in my clinical practice and found worked for me. They might work for you, too!

The strategies we will be talking about are easy to follow because we will cover each of them in detail, one by one. You are likely naturally doing many of these strategies already! But now you will have the opportunity to experience, practice, and apply these tried and tested strategies in a planned way. You will know exactly *how* to do them effectively, *why* you are using them and *when* to use them. You will learn clear information with real examples.

My hope is that you will use this information to confidently put a clear plan into practice by doing what you are already doing, with a few tweaks along the way! You will gain some skills to help kick-start and grow your connection with your child, which we know leads to more communication.

This book has been written purely for educational purposes and is not intended to replace therapy in any way. There is no guarantee that your child will take a sudden leap and start talking immediately. But simple things you change right away can have a massive impact on your child's readiness to connect with you, learn new things and communicate both now and in the future. Many parents come back to me to tell me the recommended strategies they put into practice had an immediate impact on their child in various ways they were not expecting. They tell me they noticed their child engaging more frequently, engaging for longer periods, and starting to make more attempts to make sounds or words - all while having fun.

The strategies discussed are aimed at both allistic and autistic children. You do not need a speech and language assessment in order to begin using these strategies. They have been explicitly designed so you can start creating opportunities for change and growth right away, no matter the underlying cause. The reality is that we may never find out why a child finds communication or language challenging. I take the view that it is always best to get stuck in with some strategies to make a difference now rather than potentially wasting time trying to figure out the reasons why. We can figure out what's going on later once we have put some helpful tips into place.

Some strategies in this book will resonate with you more than others, but I encourage you to explore all the tips with your child and see which ones work for your child. You are also encouraged to adapt the examples and ideas to your own child because your child may have their own unique likes and dislikes. The main idea is to only do what your child finds fun and interesting. If they are not invested in it, then they won't enjoy it or pay enough attention to connect with you.

Be sure to complete the quick challenges and the video challenges. They are there to help you put the strategies into practice for lasting change. They will also help you reflect on how they worked (or didn't work!), and how you may need to adapt them specifically for your child.

Here are a few paraphrased examples of what other parents have said when looking back at themselves in their own video challenge clips:

- *I realized that I talk a lot and I don't need to be talking all the time.*
- *I'm learning to 'catch' the moments when he is interested in something so that I can talk about that.*
- *I realized I was taking ownership of the play instead of letting* her *take ownership of it.*
- *I didn't notice that he was looking towards what I was pointing at until I watched my video back.*
- *My child usually speaks in single words. I completely missed that he said the phrase 'he's a teddy' while I was playing with him, but it was so clear when I listened back! Now I know what to listen for, so I can respond to him in real-time.*

Be consistent and persistent with the strategies – as long as your child is having fun! Just because your child doesn't respond immediately doesn't mean that what you are doing is not working under the surface. The benefits could be seen in a few days, weeks or months down the line. It's a bit like a piggy bank; each time you implement a strategy, you put a penny in. One day it might just overflow.

Do also revisit this book regularly in the future. What might work now is unlikely to continue working forever. Your child will grow and change, as will their interests, even within a few weeks. You will need to adapt what you do as your child progresses so you can stay one step ahead, keep creating fun together, and support their learning and growth. Different chapters may resonate with you each time you read or listen to them.

This is not a clinical reference book. It has not been written with other professionals in mind, although it may benefit newly qualified Speech and Language Therapists or Pathologists in whatever setting they work or anyone looking for a refresher. Learning the specialist clinical skills required to be an effective therapist with very young children and their families can take time. If this sounds like you, then I'm equally delighted to share some useful ways to structure your thinking when you approach working with young, minimally-speaking children, some of whom may have complex needs.

Please note that the term 'parent' is used to refer to any caregiver, guardian, or parent of a child.

Carolyn offers special consultations to families who would like to experience the power of live video coaching.

If you want to learn more, you can sign up for a FREE 15 minute 'Early Communication Coaching Strategy' call with Carolyn by emailing info@diyspeechtherapy.com *here:*

You can also join our online community of like-minded parents and caregivers for support at www.diyspeechtherapy.com *where you can interact with others in similar circumstances, access useful information and hear about other upcoming books, resources and courses:*

1

STRATEGY 1: GET OUT OF MY OWN HEAD!

Get out of my own head, get close, and watch my child. Sounds so simple, right? You're probably thinking: 'What is she talking about? I do this all the time!'. I guarantee that we all believe we get close to our children and pay attention to them incessantly, but the reality is that we are busy thinking about what's in our own heads most of the time; it's human nature.

We are also parents, and 'parents are supposed to teach'! We have this idea that we must teach our children to do everything. This is perfect when we think about teaching independence skills like dressing and handwashing or academic skills like writing. Whenever you are with your child, you are likely wondering, 'Right, what can I teach now?'. But communication doesn't work that way.

Communication, in the way that we use it, is a unique feature of being human. We all need connection. We like communicating our experiences to connect with others. We connect best with others when we need to share something real for a genuine reason.

Imagine yourself in a foreign country where you can't speak the language and must buy a one-way train ticket. You could learn the phrase from a phrase book to ask for it at the ticket office. If you do this, you'll remember that phrase way better and for longer than if your friend asked you to repeat that same phrase after them while sitting in your kitchen having a glass of wine over dinner! In the first scenario, you genuinely needed the ticket; it was a real message: you had to get the ticket or you would be stranded! In the second scenario, you just copied what your friend said and didn't need to communicate that message to anyone for any particular or important reason.

The same applies to 'teaching' communication: if we as parents ask our children to copy what we say, or if all they do is fill in the blanks ('the doggie says…'), then this is not sustainable and it's not natural communication. It might be temporarily fun for a while, but your child is likely to lose interest and stop doing it at some point because it is not really communicating anything genuine or leading anywhere.

So we need to find ways to get natural communication started. This is more likely to lead to genuine to-and-fro interaction. Following the strategies in sequence will help you unlearn some parent teaching habits that you may be unaware of and begin to tune into your child more and more so that you can provide a solid basis for real communication between you.

We must accept that even if we think we are already stopping what we are doing, 'getting out of my own head', getting close to our children and paying attention to them, there is always scope to do more of it so that our children can connect with us more frequently and in a way that will be more likely to lead to more communication opportunities.

When we think of 'getting out of our own head', 'getting close' or 'watching', how exactly do we do this? To do Strategy 1 effectively, ask yourself the following questions.

'GET OUT OF MY OWN HEAD' QUESTIONS:

1. Am I 'getting out of my own head' and actually stopping what I'm thinking and doing?
2. Am I close enough to my child, or can I go over and get closer to them, ideally in front of them at their eye level?
3. What is my child looking at and interested in?
4. What little movements is my child doing?
5. What little sounds is my child making?

It takes ALL your attention to do all these things. If you don't give these questions your all, it means that you are still in your own head, and that means you can't focus on your child properly. It will really help if you get used to letting go of what you had planned to do. This can be extremely difficult for most of us at the best of times!

Remember that as parents, we are hardwired to 'teach' our children – we teach them to eat by themselves with a spoon, we teach them to build a tower with blocks, and we teach them to read. But when we are 'teaching', we think our own things in our own heads, which means we have little room to pay attention to the things our children are doing or paying attention to moment by moment.

Perhaps your child usually sits on a favorite mat and plays with jigsaws. That doesn't mean that they will do the same thing next time. They might go sit by the window instead. Should you call your child back to the mat where you expected them to go and where *you* want them to go? Or should you get close to them and look to see what *they* are interested in? Yes, get close to them at the window and see what they are interested in! When you point and comment on what they are looking at, then you're setting things up for joint attention and connection.

WHAT POSITION?

When you get close to your child in this scenario we just mentioned, you will likely be beside them at the window, looking out of the window together. But if your child is focusing on a toy or object, it is more helpful to sit opposite them. You will need to pull out toy furniture like play kitchens or tables away from the wall to get behind them and be opposite your child. If your child likes lying on the floor, lie down too so you can be opposite them at their eye level. If they are sitting on the couch, kneel on the floor before them so you are at eye level. If they are sitting on the floor, you may need to lie on your front opposite them and lean on your elbows, or you can lie on your side while supporting yourself with one elbow to be at eye level with your child.

Recently, I observed a mom and her son playing together on the floor at eye level, looking at a fun cogwheel game. The child picked up his favorite cogwheel, got up and ran off around the room with it, delighted with himself. At first, the mom didn't follow him and tried to call him back, and he continued to run around happily, doing his own thing. When she 'got close' by physically moving over to him and the rest of the cogwheels, he immediately positioned himself opposite her and engaged with her. That interaction would not have happened if the mom hadn't moved closer to him at eye level. This sounds so simple, but we may not think of it in the moment.

Some children don't like it when others get too close. This is okay: in this case we need to respect their body space. You can position yourself further back at a distance they are comfortable with. They will appreciate it, and it will help them to trust you as a supportive communication partner. You can still make a difference with other strategies.

While you are trying out Strategy 1, it is VERY important to stay quiet. Don't say anything... If you start to say something, you will go back inside your own head, and that's what we are trying to avoid with Strategy 1! Give yourself time to answer the questions we mentioned above.

QUICK CHALLENGES:

1. Print or write out the 'Get Out Of My Own Head' questions with a thick dark marker on sticky notes, and stick the notes as reminders on any wall where you and your child usually go, like the kitchen, the fridge door, the play area wall. Writing out the questions will help you to process and retain the information.

2. Count to *at least* 20 slowly and quietly right now to give you a sense of how long to stay quiet and how long to watch for. Yes. We mean to wait that long. Don't jump in and try to say something when with your child. Don't assume anything! Instead, start by sitting with them *quietly*, get out of your own head, and spend time watching them. You may think you know what your child is doing, but at some point, their attention will wander to something else. If you're still 'in your own head', you may miss it, which is a missed opportunity to connect!

3. Take a minute to consider your room and the positions your child likes to be in to help set you up for maintaining the best possible eye-level positions. Will you need to move toys and furniture away from the walls? Will you need to remove some toys so it's less distracting? Write down some positions you intend to try

based on their favorite activities. Try to get into those positions now and find a way you can be both comfortable and at eye level. When you practice this, you will be helping your child to notice and engage with you more. You will also be better able to pick up on their thoughts, likes and dislikes. This will inform you how you can join in and connect with your child most successfully.

We have discussed the strategy, but why are we 'getting out of our own head', getting close and watching so intensely?

Because it means we will know what they are really interested in, moment by moment. Then we can join them in what they like at that specific moment. If they have chosen to do something, it means that they are interested in that thing they are paying attention to. When we come and sit with them and pay attention to the same thing as them, what does this remind you of ...? Joint attention! You are both now looking at the same thing together. They don't have to shift their attention, and we can get straight to work with all our strategies and support your child's ability to experience the most fun.

If your child is unaware that you are both looking at the same thing, that's okay. You are setting the scene for your child to connect and share attention jointly with you when they are ready.

If your child can already share attention jointly with you, then when you get out of your own head, get close to them and watch, you are sending them the message that they are important and that you are there for them. Your child is more likely to want to connect and share the joy with you, and we know that connection leads to communication!

Let's consider a few examples of getting 'out of your own head'. Imagine you are playing with your child's favorite toy. Your child looks sideways on the floor at a random bit of fluff, and you notice a little finger going over to investigate. Should you persist with the favorite toy or follow the finger to the bit of fluff on the floor? Yes, go with the fluff! I know it sounds silly, but you may get more fun out of the situation by noticing and saying something about the fluff rather than trying to drag your child's attention back to the toy they are no longer interested in!

What if your child is playing with little toy ducks and starts pretending to make them feed out of tiny toy buckets, but then your child discovers that two little buckets fit on their fingers and look a bit like shoes, then starts to wiggle their fingers? Go with the wiggling and focus on that! Abandon trying to 'feed the ducks' and move with what your child is focusing on and enjoying moment by moment.

This all makes sense right now as we discuss it, but I guarantee that you will miss things in real time – again, it's human nature. I miss them too! We can only pay attention to one thing at a time. It takes a lot of effort to stay focused on what they are enjoying and the sounds they are making while at the same time trying to figure out where we can take it so that we make the best use of the opportunity to have the most fun together.

When you do Strategy 1 effectively, you will notice all sorts of new things about what your child is actively thinking about moment by moment. For example, when playing with blocks, what exactly is your child actually paying attention to? Do they pay the most attention when placing the blocks on top of each other? Or is it the weight of the blocks in their hand, the way the light bounces off them, or the sound and commotion they make as they fall?

On top of that, what they pay attention to changes all the time. Just because we believe we are 'playing with the blocks' for three minutes doesn't mean your child is thinking of the blocks for those entire three minutes. Maybe they got distracted by the light flickering, the noise of a car passing by outside, the wet dog smell coming from the other room, or the feeling of their own tummy rumbling.

When you stop thinking about blocks themselves and go with what your child is thinking about and feeling, it will open up lots more opportunities for your child to connect with you instead of you trying to pull your child's attention back to the blocks over and over.

'GET OUT OF MY OWN HEAD!' VIDEO CHALLENGE

It's time to set you your first video challenge! This strategy applies to children of all levels, whether your child is not speaking yet, is minimally speaking, or is already using words. You are going to record yourself and your child on your smartphone (or another suitable device) for two or three minutes. Go and sit with your child quietly. Make sure that both you and your child are captured in the frame. Having someone else video you from the side is a good idea. That way, during the replay, you get to see yourself, your child, and whatever activity they are involved in. It doesn't matter if the activity is physical; for example, if they are running around, you can follow them and get active, too!

During the recording, you will try to get out of your own head, get close to your child and watch them for that whole time without saying anything. Do not speak. If you like to chat, this may be challenging for you, but you can do it! You can smile and nod instead.

This video challenge may be harder than it sounds. What are the challenges you will be faced with? You may forget to get close enough to your child and you might call them back to you instead. You may be tempted to join in or say things – don't! Just follow The questions 1-5 above that you wrote out and stick to the plan.

This is your chance to practice noticing the little things. Take notice of everything you see your child do and hear your child say. You are not trying to get involved yet. Do this challenge anyway, even if you feel your child already connects well with you: you will likely learn something about yourself just as much as about your child. Just watch and listen and drink it all in!

Stop here and do not continue until you have completed your first Video Challenge.

Now you are done recording yourself and your child, read the questions below and watch your recording back in full.

1. Did you remember to get out of your own head?
2. Did you really pay attention to what your child was looking at and figure out what they might be thinking from moment to moment?
3. Did you get close enough to your child?
4. What sounds and movements did you notice? And what did you learn that you might otherwise have missed?
5. Did you miss any of your child's little sounds or attempts to say or communicate something?
6. Did your child react differently than usual because you were quieter and more present? In what way?

7. Did they notice you, interact with you or communicate with you in some way?

You can write your reflections here:

____

____

____

____

Well done! You have attempted one of the most important strategies to make a difference to your child's ability to connect and communicate with you. If this is something you found challenging or if you found you had a completely different experience watching yourself back to what you thought was happening live, you may wish to repeat this video practice many times before you move on.

I would encourage you to do this practice on consecutive days for at least a week. Record yourself every day for two to three minutes. Then watch back and compare your live experience to your experience reviewing your recording. Be proud of yourself, and congratulate yourself if you began to notice some things live in the moment that you might otherwise have missed before. You may have someone else watch you live and review your recording with you, so they can give you feedback on whether they thought you were getting 'out of your own head' and if you were going with what your child was actually interested in from moment to moment.

When you record yourself in this way and notice something you might otherwise miss, you will know what to look out for next time!

Strategy 1: Summary

In his chapter, we learned...

- that we need to get out of our own head and focus on a child's experiences - it's all about *them*
- we need to get physically close to a child, as long as they are happy for us to do so, and this means following them around while we work on this strategy!
- to stay quiet while we watch what they are interested in moment by moment
- that eye-level positions can help provide a good basis for watching to getting into a child's head, and help nurture interaction and joint attention
- to stop trying to 'teach' language because this doesn't address authentic natural conversational language
- when getting started, stay quiet and count slowly to 20 to give you the space and time to adjust and pick up on your child's specific interest at that moment
- what interests them could be unexpected or unusual, like noticing fluff on the ground, and later on we can add communication to these unexpected interests

2

STRATEGY 2: GET INVOLVED AND HAVE FUN!

Now you have learned to 'get out of your own head' and focus on your child properly, you can start to 'Get Involved and Have Fun' with your child! Having fun is the easiest way to connect with your child, and we know that connection leads to.... Communication.

LOOK FOR FUN MOMENTS

Look for moments of fun that you can get involved in. For some children, this could include repetitive activities they often like to do, like lining things up or moving things from one place to another and back again. They might enjoy looking at things in certain ways or listening to interesting sounds. Other children might like playing games based on movement or sensory experiences like slides, chasing or tickling. Or there could be something intriguing or new that your child takes an interest in, like when a toy falls off the table and makes a funny sound, or they might like how the paper feels and sounds when they rip it up.

Some children might be drawn to toy-based play with favourite toys, dolls, teddies, toy characters, toy vehicles or animals. Look for what they want to do with the toy, even if it is not what you normally do with it! For example, holding up and looking through the stacking rings like glasses instead of building the tower with them.

Opportunities could also arise when something goes wrong, like when you're getting ready to go out and their hat falls forward by accident over their face (this could make a great 'peekaboo' game!) or when something silly happens like when they try to put a brick that is too big into a small cart ('Oh no! It's too big!').

IT'S NOT ABOUT NARRATION

Sometimes parents may be advised to 'narrate your child's experiences'. This means constantly talking in the background about what your child is doing, narrating every little thing they do: 'You put the red block on, you took the blue block off, you're getting the yellow block, you're putting the green brick on'. Suppose your tone is neutral, and you're just chatting away like it is background noise. In that case, that's exactly what your narration will be. Your child will likely think, 'This is background noise' or 'This is something my parent does and has little relevance to me'. They might even learn to ignore some of it. Either way it probably will not lead to 'to-and-fro' interaction.

Whereas if you focus your moments of connection on the little events that have meaning for your child.... Ding! Your child will have a lightbulb moment and connect with you and any language you have just said. The moment comes to life!

We don't need to talk constantly - we only really need to give language for the significant events as they experience them. Keep the ordinary chat to a minimum. Sometimes, we can clutter things up with back-to-back comments and questions. When we do this, a child doesn't have the headspace to process everything. We want to limit irrelevant chat and choose key moments of interest. Then, what we say will stand out more and is more likely to grab their interest, plus they are more likely to connect their thoughts with your words.

WHEN TO GET INVOLVED

Remember that Strategy 2 happens in the moments right after you have done Steps 1-5 from Strategy 1 and waited long enough (at least 20-30 seconds). Once you have truly noticed your child's interest in something, we need to discuss what that 'something' could be in more detail.

As parents who like to 'teach', we tend to focus on conventional play. We naturally want to teach our children how to do standard play activities, like blocks, shape sorters, puzzles, construction toys, dolls, tea sets, and a play kitchen, as examples.

But standard play activities are now irrelevant in our plan to create more opportunities to connect and communicate, in the sense that 'normal' play activities don't specifically feature on our 'to-do' list when we think about getting an interaction started.

If you sit down with your child and say, 'Come on! Let's do the blocks! Do you think you are 'getting out of your own head'? No, you're probably still in your own head, looking for your child to follow your plan, leading the play with things you want your child to do! This is not a wrong thing to do in and of itself. But we are here to find opportunities for connection and communication.

If your child happens to want to do the blocks right now, yay! You may succeed in starting up a 'to and fro' interaction. But research has found it is much more effective to promote connection and communication by joining in with what a child wants or is thinking of and following that. That is what they are enjoying or intrigued by right now. This may not be a conventional 'activity' or 'play'. In a previous example, we mentioned a child becoming interested in fluff on the floor by glancing at it and moving a finger towards it – this is a valid thing to communicate about if that happens to be the thing capturing your child's attention at that moment! I know it sounds crazy, but fluff really can get an interaction started.

Remember what happened in a previous example with the toy ducks and buckets: The mom stopped trying to feed the ducks when her daughter put the buckets on her fingers and wiggled them. Because her mum responded to her interest by copying the wiggling and talking about walking instead, her child was intrigued and delighted. They were focused on the same thing, which we know promotes joint attention.

Another child liked tearing tiny bits of paper off a toilet roll, much to the dismay of his parents initially. But his dad joined in and ripped little bits of toilet roll off too. This led to natural turn-taking, where each took turns ripping bits of paper off. His son noticed him and really enjoyed the connection with his dad. As a result, he stayed engaged for longer than usual.

Another mom sat on the floor opposite her young boy on the couch, stacking cups into each other. He was picking one up at a time, turning it around and looking at it, so the mum joined in with her own set and did the same thing as him in real-time, just like a mirror. He noticed her and smiled, then started to change what he did to check if his mom was really doing the same thing.

A dad sat on the floor trying to call his son over to play with him. His son wandered over to the window. Instead of calling him back to the mat, his dad followed him to the window and got close to him. The dad started pointing at what he thought his son was looking at: the family car, a neighbor's house, and grass. He commented by saying, 'Look at the car! That's Julie's house! There's the grass!'. This helped his son connect with him as they were now both looking at the same thing and enjoying that moment together.

Don't be concerned if your child happens to like messy play. You won't be indulging or spoiling them. This is just what they need to do right now. You will be turning these situations into a shared experience with a chance to connect, which we know leads to…? Yes! Communication. Any mess to clean up later will be worth it.

COPYING

A simple strategy you can use to get involved is to copy or imitate what your child does. We have already seen some examples of this above, with the dad who copied ripping off tiny bits of toilet paper and the mom who copied stacking cups. Copying is a great way to start an interaction with a child who is minimally speaking and mainly communicating to ask for things they want or showing they don't want something. It is also a great way to start a 'conversation' if your child already uses some sounds or words. It is vital to figure out what your child is actually interested in doing at that moment first, like lining up cars or trains, looking at something from different angles, lying on the floor, jumping, playdough, coloring, playing teddy, building a tower of bricks or examining that bit of fluff on the floor!

These are all things that children may be interested in doing, but some are not considered the usual type of play we expect. But they are things you can join in with and do exactly as your child does in real-time, just like a mirror!

You can copy your child's physical movements: when your child lifts an arm up, you lift your arm up in time with them. You can also copy any sounds they make, even little grunts or squeals. When you do this, wait until your child has finished making their sound first before you copy them - that way, you are making it into a fun to-and-fro activity. For example, if your child lets out a big sigh, you let out a big sigh right away after they finish sighing!

You can line up your own line of things, pick something up to look at in the same way as your child, or lie on the floor when your child does and roll when they do! Your child may love that you copy exactly what they do in real-time. They may notice you more, be intrigued, and check to see if you really are copying them. This is precisely the goal of copying. It can be a great way to get a fun interaction going, especially with children who often prefer to play alone

When copying, don't just copy one of your child's actions and then stop. You need to copy at least 20-30 actions and sounds in real time over a span of a few minutes.

HAVE MY OWN SET

If your child chooses to play with objects or toys, you can copy by having two similar sets. You can use one set while your child is using the other so you can copy them in real-time.

You may try to copy them using the same toys, but it doesn't have to be exactly the same toy or object: you could use something of a similar size and function. For example, if your child likes putting coins in an electronic piggy bank toy (and you only have one piggy bank), you can sit across from your child and put shapes into a shape sorter. Or if your child is dropping their favorite plastic characters into water, you could drop plastic bricks into the water. Remember: it is your child's actions and sounds you are copying, so the objects or toys you have don't matter as long as they allow you to mimic your child's actions.

Some children may become upset if you take the toys they're playing with to copy them with or if you use other favorite toys of theirs. It may look like emotion or pickiness on the outside, but this reflects what could be a very uncomfortable feeling on the inside for them. It may be equivalent to someone asking us to sleep on the left side of the bed when we have slept on the right side for years, and we know we won't be able to sleep! So when you take a toy to copy with, it might feel like you are taking their favorite thing ever. For some, it could feel like their safety blanket is being taken away.

How can we get involved and connect in this kind of scenario, and should we get involved at all?

For example, suppose your child likes cars and finds it difficult to tolerate you handling their cars when you try to join in and copy. In that case, sit a little further away so you won't bother your child by getting in their space. You can find different objects of a similar size or shape that you can use to copy your child's *movements* or *sounds.* The objects don't need to be identical. So for the example of the cars, you could copy your child's actions with blocks instead. This means your child may not be emotionally attached enough to your blocks to become upset or want to take the blocks off you. But your child might still notice that you are copying their actions and sounds and glance over to check out what you are doing. This is a great step!

If your child takes the toys you have away from you, then they may let you pick up the one they dropped so you can keep the copying game going. You may end up swapping the toys back and forth, and that's okay! You're still involved in a fun game with interaction.

We are trying to find ways to encourage them to notice and connect with you. Our goal is to become part of the game in a fun way. But if your child doesn't like it or it upsets them, then stop and take a step back. Your child may need to play in their own way for a while to help them stay calm and happy. You will know to back off if they are playing by themselves and ignore you or if they get upset when you try to get involved or try to copy even with your own set. If this is the case, then it's okay for you to abandon using this type of activity as a time for learning and just let them play in whatever way they are comfortable. This activity may be their 'down time', in the same way that we may need quiet time after a long day at work. You can sit somewhere they are happy for you to sit and make fun sounds to join in, as in Strategy 7 on Sound Effects. You can also go back to Strategies 1 and 2. You can also explore Strategy 6 on Short Repeatable Games for ideas on fun physical activities that could turn into enjoyable, predictable shared play instead.

For children who can already share joint attention with you or are starting to use words, it can be intriguing to them when you begin to copy them. They may glance and notice you. This can lead to natural turn-taking and interaction. They might start to take charge or lead with new actions and check if you are really copying them! They might change what they do slightly and see if you get it right, or they might say something, vocalize with sounds, or comment with words.

For example, if your child likes to jump and you join in, they might start to notice by looking at you. Then they might slow down or go faster, and watch if you slow down or speed up, too! They might stop and put their arms out to see if you'll copy that. They might try out some sounds ('*ah!*'), or if your child has some words, they might give you a command by saying '*stop!*' or '*go!*' or something similar.

Or if your child likes to bang things like their spoon on the table at snack time, join in with your own spoon. Copy their rhythm in real-time. See if your child likes it or responds and if you can start to take turns banging. Focus on taking turns naturally so that a 'to and fro' interaction might organically emerge out of it! It doesn't matter if your child is unaware they are taking turns. By copying them, you are showing them how to take turns. In time, they will start to get the idea.

Perhaps your child enjoys playing with toys in the ways we usually expect, like putting cars on a car slide or shapes in a shape sorter. When you start to copy, these activities lend themselves well to taking natural turns. Don't just tip out all the pieces on the floor. If the pieces are everywhere, your child will be busy looking at all the pieces. It will be hard for them to focus on you! Having all the pieces in a bag or container can be helpful. You are suddenly part of that game when you can take one or two out at a time and hand them to your child.

Another tip is to have only one or two cars out. There will be less distraction, and your child will be better able to pay attention to what's happening and the language spoken! As one car goes down the slide, you can pick up the one that is already at the bottom. Then, you will have an endless supply of cars to keep handing your child. If your child is adamant that they want to pick it up and use it, let them and get another car ready in your hand to give them when the original car is getting near the bottom of the slide. They might take your car to put on the car slide, and you are now part of the activity again. Gather up spare cars as long as your child is calm, and you'll have more cars to offer them over and over as long as they stay interested.

If your child enjoys pretending games, then copying can still be fun: For example, pretending to speak on the phone, playing tea party, putting teddy to bed, or fixing teddy with the doctor's set. These are great activities for when your child is ready! You may encourage a natural to-and-fro in play routines by copying them 'talking' on the phone, taking turns pouring tea, putting teddy to bed, or fixing teddy when he has 'hurt' himself.

If your child is at this stage, they will likely easily engage with you already, so you don't need to work to get an interaction going. You can move forward with new strategies to promote communication. You can still try copying just for fun, but Strategies 3 and 4 will be particularly relevant. At this stage, it's not all about following them. Once they are ready, you can introduce new fun play and new ideas that you know they will likely enjoy. This is most effective when your child has reached the stage of sharing joint attention with you and is already showing interest in copying you. But let them explore the toys themselves first to see if it is something that they like.

QUICK CHALLENGE

Make a list of the activities and games your child enjoys that you could join in and copy, like a mirror in real-time. Add to your list the types of sounds your child might make during play. Put the list up somewhere where you will see it to remind you to get involved and copy your child's actions and sounds!

'GET INVOLVED AND HAVE FUN!' VIDEO CHALLENGE

Read the instructions below carefully, then record yourself and your child again for two to three minutes. Capture both you and your child in the frame so you can see what you both did and said when you look back at the recording. Make sure when the video starts to roll that you do Strategy 1 first for at least 30 seconds:

- Get out of your own head
- Get close to your child and
- Watch your child quietly

While you are watching, try to spot what it is that your child is interested in. Fluff? The way the wallpaper is peeling? The sound of the ice cream truck passing by? Or they may want to play with a toy in a way you were expecting. They may want to play in an unexpected way, like examining the tail of the monkey rather than wanting to say, '*Ooh ooh ooh!*'.

Now that you have spotted what they are thinking about or what they are interested in, it is the right time to get involved and have fun! Talk about and point to what your child is actually interested in: '*Wow! Look! That's so fluffy/silly/long/cool!*'. Then wait. Be natural, do what you do best as a parent and have fun! You can make something fun happen that might encourage your child to giggle or laugh. Then, as soon as you have said something, start again at the beginning and repeat the process:

- Wait and Watch
- What are they interested in?
- Can you copy their sounds or movements?
- Comment and point in a fun way
- Wait and Watch

- What are they interested in?
- Can you copy their sounds or movements?
- Comment and point in a fun way

It's that simple. Remember: it's all about your child, not you! While you are waiting, you will be giving yourself time to watch and notice small things you might otherwise miss:

If your child is touching something with their finger, they are exploring what it feels like. So you can copy as long as they tolerate it and say something to describe it: '*Oh! It's so smooth / fluffy!*'.

If they are looking at a detail on the wheel of an upside-down train and turning the wheel around, you could point and say: '*Ooh! Round and round and round!*'.

If they start moving their body when you are sitting down together, become aware of it and 'read' what you think they might want to do. Do they want to go? Then say, 'Let's go!' and take their hand to lead them away because that is likely what your child is thinking. If you try to drag them back to the activity, you'll be back inside your own head. But you are trying to get inside their head and out of your own.

If your child makes sounds, copy what you hear, even if it doesn't make any sense. You might get a lovely 'to and fro' going where your child says something, and then you say something. Your child may continue taking turns with you, making various fun sounds back and forth.

If you catch yourself going back into your own head, stop, take a moment and watch them again. Try to catch those little moments or openings for you to get into their head and figure out exactly what they might be thinking. Guaranteed, it's probably not what you thought it would be before you started watching them!

Stop now and do not read on until you have completed this video exercise to help you practice this strategy. Record yourself interacting with your child for a few minutes now, following the instructions above. Then, come back and review your video using the questions below.

Great! Now you are done, look back at your video. Try to find moments when you 'got out of your own head', got close to your child, watched and listened.

1. Did you wait and watch long enough to spot something they were actually thinking about?
2. Find moments when you spotted something fun to get involved in.
3. What was the fun thing?

Write your reflections here:

Now look back at your video again.

1. Did you get involved? How?
2. Did you copy your child?'
3. What did you say or do?
4. How did your child react?
5. In what ways did your child show signs of connecting with you? Did they move their body, change their facial expression, notice you, or some other way?
6. What worked best to get them to notice or engage with you? Was it waiting? Or when you made fun sounds or comments?
7. Did you get to comment and point to what your child was thinking about?
8. How did your child react overall?
9. Now that you are reflecting on the interaction, what else could you have tried?

Note your thoughts here:

____

____

____

____

Learn to catch yourself when you get back into your own head. This will really help your connection with your child because you'll be focusing on what *they* like and think of instead of spending energy trying to get them to focus on what is in *your* head, what *you* want them to play with, or calling them back to something they have already finished with.

Practice this every day for at least one week. If you need to spend longer practicing Strategy 2, keep recording yourself daily and review your recordings as per the video challenge until you feel comfortable joining in with the fun, copying, making comments and pointing. Once you have mastered this strategy, you'll be ready for the next one!

Strategy 2: Summary

In this chapter you learned...

- to look for fun moments to join in with. to look for and prioritize authentic communication opportunities
- the best time to get involved is once we have truly noticed what a child's interest is, moment by moment
- to watch for and copy unconventional play or comment on an unexpected momentary interest that grabs a child's attention
- following their unexpected or messy interests is not indulging them - these are great opportunities for connection, interaction, and communication
- constant background narration or chatter is not the best strategy to support connection, interaction, or communication
- mirroring movements in real-time, and copying sounds in turn can be gateways to back-and-forth interaction
- when copying, finding a separate set of objects to copy with can be helpful. The focus is copying your child's sounds and physical movements like a mirror in real-time, so the objects don't matter
- tips for becoming part of the game by offering desired objects naturally during play
- to watch and wait, notice their interest, copy them, comment and point, then repeat the process

3

STRATEGY 3: LISTEN. REALLY LISTEN!

We have spent a lot of time talking about watching and listening already, but we will spend some time thinking about how and why we must listen so carefully.

Most parents say they want their child to talk using words. But when working with children with communication needs, we take a 'total communication' approach. This means we accept any communication on their first attempt, no matter how they choose to communicate with us. Suppose a child communicates something, and we understand their message or know what they are trying to say. In that case, we never withhold or wait for them to achieve 'better' communication to give them what they want. We must honor their first attempt, even if we know they can communicate it in a more advanced way.

For example, a child who isn't using words yet, but can point and reach for things, hands their parent a jar for them to open. Should the parent wait for the child to communicate in a 'better' way by pointing or reaching? No, the child has already communicated that they need help to open it when they handed it to their parent in the first place. So, waiting for the child to ask in a 'better' way is not honoring their first attempt. As soon as your child hands you a jar, you could say, 'Let's open it!' as you open it for them right away and then hand it back to them or the contents. Noticing the first communication attempt may take some practice, so you can revisit this if this sounds like your child's stage.

It is important to say the words at the same time as you open the jar so your child can pair the words with the action. This helps your child to develop their understanding of language.

Another child who can use short phrases like, '*Open the box*' might hand you the jar and say '*Open*' instead of, '*Open the jar*'. Would you stop and not open the jar and wait for them to say it in the 'better' way? No: Once they have said '*Open*', you can respond immediately with something like, '*Okay! Let's open the jar!*', as you open it for them and hand it back to them.

Now you may ask, 'Well, how will my child learn to talk then? Won't they always take the easy option?' This is a very valid question.

Think back to our earlier example of working for a boss – the one who listened patiently to you, accepted your conversation without judgment, and made you feel like you wanted to chat more, remember?

So what does this mean for our children? We need to accept all forms of communication on their first attempt because it helps them to:

- Feel validated
- Know that they are important no matter what way they try to connect with you

- Know that no matter what, you will hear them, and their message will be received
- Feel that communication is easy
- Trust in you as a communication partner
- Feel like they want to do more of it
- Doing more of it gives them more opportunities to expand and practice new ways to communicate when they are ready

The idea that we want our children to experience communication as something easy is crucial for them to want to do more of it.

If we don't respond to their first attempt to communicate, and if we insist on them communicating it in a better way instead, then we are effectively telling them, 'The way you did that wasn't good enough'.

What might the long-term impact of this be on your child?...

It is the opposite of everything we just said above:

- Your child might not feel like their attempt has been validated
- They feel like their message wasn't important
- That there is a specific and 'difficult' way that they are supposed to communicate with you
- Their trust in you as a communication partner will wane
- They will start to feel like the effort is pointless and will be less inclined to want to try to communicate something to you next time.

We need to watch, listen, and recognize those little attempts to communicate that we may normally miss and catch them as they happen in real-time. We need to try and respond to whatever way our child communicates with us on their first attempt.

What exactly are we looking for? Your child could initiate interaction or communication with you in many different ways.

COMMUNICATION REPERTOIRE

Here is a Communication Repertoire to help you identify how your child might communicate with you. The communication could either be unintentional or directed to you on purpose. To use a total communication approach we are going to accept all of these ways as something we can respond to:

1. Stop what they are doing, quieten
2. Change facial expression
3. Physically move closer to the item they want
4. Accept something from me when I hand it to them
5. Move their body (lean in towards me, jump or wriggle)
6. Make an unintentional sound with their voice (sneeze, cough, laugh, sigh, other little vocal sounds, or loud sounds)
7. Reach for something they want
8. Notice me by glancing at me
9. Notice what I'm doing with my hands
10. Take me by the hand and lead me to what they want
11. Reach out their hand to take something from me
12. Hand me something
13. Physically move my hand to make something happen or operate something
14. Follow my point by glancing when I point something out either nearby on a picture or to something further away outside

15. Indicate their choice by looking, reaching, or making sounds when presented with options
16. Point with their whole hand towards something they want
17. Point with a pointing finger
18. Make an intentional sound, hum a song, vocalize or use chatter
19. Copy sounds, intonation (the music of the voice), a word or words someone else just said
20. Copy sounds, words or phrases they have previously heard at a much later time
21. Use a word or words spontaneously
22. Combine two or more of these ways of communicating simultaneously, which is more advanced than doing just one form of communication at a time; for example, making sounds and reaching simultaneously
23. Use combinations of words to make phrases
24. Add anything that your own child does that is not covered here ______________________________

Later, you will have a Video Challenge to help you identify all the various ways your child communicates. When you are listening and watching, you'll write down exactly what your child is doing with their body, face, and hands, and you'll listen out for their sounds or word attempts. This will help you get to know your child's communication repertoire and recognize when and how to respond.

QUICK CHALLENGE

You can print out or write out the Communication Repertoire above now to help guide your practice when you look back at your challenge videos.

THE POWER OF SOUNDS

Children can make two kinds of sounds: intentional and unintentional sounds. When a child makes an intentional sound, they send you a message on purpose, whether you understand it or not. But children often make random, unintentional sounds with no clear message or obvious specific purpose.

If your child is non-speaking or minimally speaking, these little unintentional random sounds your child makes are incredibly important. As parents, we can get so caught up watching *how* our child plays or communicates that we sometimes forget to listen out for the littlest sounds they make. Or else we only listen out for clear, well-formed words and screen out all their unclear vocalizations and chatter.

Very often, when reviewing videos of themselves, parents tell me that they completely missed instances when their child was copying the tone of their voice (intonation) or trying to say a word they had never heard them try before. This means a missed opportunity for those parents to respond.

We want to take notice of the sounds your child makes because this is how we can show them the power of their own voice. To truly take a total communication approach, we want to help support them in their attempts to communicate in new ways to empower them. Self-agency is an incredibly important goal for all children. We want children to be able to advocate for themselves in whatever way they can. Of course, children do not need speech to learn self-agency and learn how to express themselves. However, we do want to give them a chance to explore the power of their own voice to make things happen in the world and with the people around them.

This means we must listen very carefully and respond immediately to both the intentional and unintentional sounds our children make, where possible. If we re-establish the balance and make their voice of equal importance to respond to, then we let them know that using their voice is an equally if not more immediate and effective way to communicate needs and wants to others. We can do this by responding to their little sounds and attempts. Even if they make unintentional random sounds, try to pick up on them as they happen and react to them immediately. This can take a lot of practice but is an incredibly powerful support for your child.

You can show your child their voice is important by using the suggestions we discuss later. It will help them make the connection that their voice is powerful, that they are a powerful force in the world and can make things happen by using their voice.

The unintentional sounds we are talking about can be anything: a random sigh, a hum, a cough, a grumble and squeal, a yawn, a giggle, vowel sounds like 'ah', 'eh' or 'ee'. You might hear your child make these sounds, but it is so easy to miss these moments as opportunities to respond to! But when you 'get out of your own head' and pay full attention to your child, you will have a better chance of picking up on these little random sounds. You can think quickly in the moment and respond in whatever way is fun for your child.

We are not advocating that you ignore other ways your child tries to communicate, like when they look at you, reach for something, or move their body – respond to everything! Remember that we use a total communication approach and always try to respond to their *first* attempt to communicate a message, whether that is physically or using their voice.

But you can make a point of focusing on their random sounds that you might otherwise miss. Then, you can quickly and naturally respond.

What might happen when you start to react to their unintentional random sounds? When we respond immediately to a sound or vocalization, even if it was unintended on your child's part, we are sending them these messages:

- That their voice is important
- That their sounds have been heard
- That their message has been received even if you don't understand it
- That you are trying your best to understand
- That you are listening and ready to act on whatever sounds they make
- That they have another means of communication at their disposal
- That using their voice with others can be fun!

Remember, we never deny if they have already expressed something. Imagine your child has already communicated something without words. In that case, we don't wait for them to say it again in a 'better' way or with words. If you expect more, it means you are getting back into your own head, and it would not be honoring your child's original communication attempt.

Imagine yourself in a restaurant. You want to ask for the check. You make the international sign by catching the eye of the waiter and 'writing' in the air or on your palm to show you need the check. The waiter comes over. Would he wait for you to say, 'Can I have the check please?' and not give you the check until you have said the actual phrase? No! He'd immediately know what you want. He would likely give you a nod and come over with the check ready to go.

How does this apply to your child? For example, if your child sees their cracker in your hand, looks, and reaches towards it at snack time, is it fair to wait longer and see if you can 'get them to say it'? No! They have already communicated what they want by looking and reaching for it, so let them have it! There will be other opportunities for them to ask for things in new ways. You want to avoid getting into a tug of war above all else.

'LISTEN' VIDEO CHALLENGE

It's time to record yourself interacting with your child again for two to three minutes as before. Always start with the earlier strategies when practicing a new video exercise unless the instructions say otherwise. Make sure you:

- Get out of your own head
- Get close
- Watch your child quietly for 30 seconds
- Figure out what they are interested in moment to moment
- Get involved and have fun!
- Then LISTEN and pay special attention to your child's little sounds.

Don't continue until you have completed this challenge. When you come back, review your video and ask yourself the questions below.

Fantastic! Now look back at your video and pay specific attention to your child's little sounds or words if they can already say some:

1. Look at the Communication Repertoire and tick off all the ways your child communicated. You may notice some ways to communicate not listed in the Communication Repertoire - write them down, too. This will give you a good idea of what you can expect from your child.
2. Did you notice any little unintentional sounds you may have missed when interacting with your child in real-time?
3. What kinds of sounds did they make with their voice?
4. Were they flexing their voice up and down?
5. Did their voice sound speech-like without actual words?
6. Or if your child can say words, what did they say? Did you miss any of their word attempts in the moment?

You can write your reflections here:

It is not uncommon to miss sounds and word attempts. Your child may likely be making more attempts than you realize. I recommend you practice this video challenge several times, ideally every day over the next week, at least 7 to 10 times. This will help you tune into your child's attempts even more. Tuning in is crucial, especially if you think your child is not yet using intentional vocalizations or sounds. You need to become aware of the unintentional sounds they make so you can respond to them more. This will encourage your child to want to try to say more things.

One tip you can try is to make a conscious effort to watch your child's mouth more. Watching their mouth may help you notice your child's little sounds and word attempts in real-time that you might otherwise miss.

Strategy 3: Summary

In this chapter, you learned...

- the importance of accepting your child's first response
- to build trust as a communication partner
- how to help your child realize the power of their voice
- your child has a repertoire of various ways that they use to communicate
- communication can either be unintentional or directed to you on purpose, but we respond to both ways regardless
- you should have a list of the various ways your child communicates, and this will guide you as to how you can realistically expect your child to communicate with you
- you can add to your child's repertoire as they include new ways to communicate

4

STRATEGY 4: RESPOND WITH ENTHUSIASM!

This strategy is all about what you can do now that you have tuned in properly and joined in with what your child is enjoying moment by moment. First, you must watch and wait for your child to do or say something listed in the Communication Repertoire. You can add your child's specific way of communicating to the list. Once your child has communicated, it's time to Respond with Enthusiasm!

Before we continue, I'd like to put in a caveat here. The 'Respond with Enthusiasm' strategy features here because many non-speaking or minimally speaking children enjoy it when others around them speak in an animated or enthusiastic way. Also, some children are under-sensitive to certain sounds and may not respond to a speaker's normal voice. As a result, it makes sense to be animated and enthusiastic!

For a small number of children, however, enthusiasm and noise can be upsetting, so if you use the 'Respond with Enthusiasm' strategy and you notice that it has an adverse effect on your child, you may need to use a different strategy and tone it down rather than up. Your child may need your voice to sound calm and reassuring to stay regulated. So instead of reading 'Respond with Enthusiasm', you'll replace it with 'Respond with *Gentleness*' and adjust your practice.

But for the rest of us, we can follow the 'Respond with Enthusiasm' strategy as laid out in this chapter.

HOW TO RESPOND

So we have already talked a bit about 'responding,' but how exactly should you respond when your child does or says something? Cheering and clapping when your child does or says something new is very tempting because it's always a very exciting moment! But neither clapping nor cheering involves natural communication.

Imagine you are back in the restaurant. You are enjoying your dinner, and when you have taken your last bite, the waiter comes over and claps... In fact, the whole restaurant stands up and claps! This would be super weird. In real life, the waiter might be delighted inside, but he would come over and ask you genuinely, '*Did you enjoy your meal?*' to which you'd reply with a real answer, '*Yes, it was lovely, thanks!*'. So we must ensure that the messages we send our children are authentic too, even if we feel like jumping up and down with joy!

What message might it be sending your child in the long run if you cheer and make a huge fuss when they do or say something new? Think about it for a minute. In our restaurant example, the whole restaurant stood up and cheered.

Does that mean they must have been watching you the entire time? Ugh!

Does it also mean they were judging your eating performance? Ugh!

How does the thought of that make you feel? Clapping and cheering are supposed to feel good! So why does this scenario not feel right? No one likes to feel like their actions are being judged, even when they achieve something good!

But a really positive interaction with someone can make us feel good without ever feeling judged. We are accepted for who we are – just like when the waiter came over in the real-life scenario, and you expressed your appreciation. You probably felt good after that because you knew it made him happy, but there was no expectation that you had to say anything specific. You volunteered it.

We want your child to volunteer communication too, when they are ready to. It is much more powerful for them to gain the trust and confidence to attempt communication again and again when the desire to communicate comes from within themselves.

Responding with Enthusiasm when your child does or says something involves all the emotions you might feel at that moment and packages it into a genuine, meaningful response. It helps your child to want to initiate communication more because your child's reactions are not under scrutiny. You are accepting any and all reactions whenever they make them.

THE 4 POINT PLAN

We can expand this strategy into four steps:

1. LISTEN
2. ACKNOWLEDGE
3. MODEL AND SHOW
4. GIVE IT (IF POSSIBLE)

1. LISTEN

We have talked about listening already. Our aim is to acknowledge those little sounds, word attempts or physical communication attempts, and model an appropriate phrase to suit the situation. When we 'listen', we watch for any reaction from the Communication Repertoire. Listen carefully to both the intentional and unintentional sounds or word attempts your child makes so that you can be ready to respond to them quickly and with enthusiasm. Remember you will also watch out for their physical attempts at communicating and accept their 'first attempt', whatever way that may be.

If your child is non-speaking or minimally speaking but can make sounds, then you need to pay particular attention to the sounds they make.

You may fall into the trap of only scanning for the physical ways they communicate with you (like moving their body or hands) because these stand out more, and you might forget to listen out for their unintentional sounds! I recommend recording yourself and your child playing together, and when you watch it back, count how many little noises and vocalizations you missed. Guaranteed, you will miss some because we can only focus on one thing at a time, and lots could happen when a child is busy having fun!

'Listening' sounds easier than it actually is for many reasons: Some of us hear everything and don't filter out sounds. But many of us spend our lives screening out unwanted sounds like car alarms, refrigerator sounds, or background noise in cafés. Either way, it is highly likely you are missing some of your child's valuable sounds: I miss sounds too, all the time. With practice, it is possible to get into the habit of picking up on your child's attempts for a few planned minutes every day and responding to more of them.

If you notice that you regularly miss the sounds your child makes in your video challenges, then go back to Strategy 3 and spend extra time focusing on detecting their sounds in real-time.

2. ACKNOWLEDGE

'Acknowledge' means you do something to show that their sound or physical communication attempt has been received:

- You can nod your head and smile. Combine this with one of the next two points:
- You could say something like '*Yeah!*', '*That's right!*', '*Cool!*', '*Really!*' or '*Wow!*'
- If your child makes some sounds, but you are unsure what your child is trying to say, you could also copy your child's sounds exactly as they have said them, with enthusiasm
- You could respond in the moment with something you might naturally say, for example: You could say, '*Yes, it is funny!*' if your child laughs

Don't worry too much if you don't understand their message. You will still let them know their voice or communication attempt is important by being present. They will notice the efforts and that you are doing your best to understand.

For example, if your child likes playing 'tickles', you could tickle them in a fun way, then pull your hands back, hovering them over your child, freeze and look excitedly at them. Wait for a couple of seconds to build fun anticipation! Then, if your child happens to make a sound, gesture, or move their body, arm or hand in some way to ask for more, you can smile, nod, and say, '*Ok! Let's do some more tickles!*'. If they don't respond after a few seconds, tickle them anyway! And say something fun like '*Tickle tickle tickle... Stop!*'.

You don't need to ask the question: 'Do you want some more tickles?' because they have already communicated that they wanted more when they moved their body or made a sound or gesture! And if they haven't done anything to ask for more, they will soon make the link that they are in charge when they move their body or make sounds and suddenly find themselves with more fun tickles!

So by responding 'as if' they used words, you are showing them that their little ways to communicate are important, and they will want to do more and more of this. Over time, their attempts will become more and more intentional and closer to clear gestures or sounds or even words later on.

You are likely doing much of this already, but the difference is that now you will be watching and responding in a planned, more consistent way so that your child feels not only heard but there will also be a trusted consequence to their attempts, some of which you may previously have missed. You have a repertoire to look back over. You should now know all the ways you can expect your child to communicate, and you'll notice when they experiment with new ways so you'll be quick to respond.

Remember that our goal is to encourage them to want to communicate more, so when you take an active role by acknowledging all attempts on their first go, you are helping them to feel like communication is positive, effective, and fun! Even if you know that your child can 'say it a better way', don't ask them to say it again. They have already communicated, so listen, acknowledge, model and show, and move on. There will be other opportunities for your child to shine and show what they can do or say!

3. MODEL AND SHOW

Imagine you have done Strategies 1, 2, and 3. You think you know what your child is thinking as they move, make their sound(s), or attempt a word or gesture. Now, you can put their message into the words *they* could ideally say when ready. This is what we call *modeling*: We give them the relevant words so they can pair those words to the situation and learn what those words mean. Eventually, they might even say the words, but we do not expect them to say anything at this point! Our goal is to say the words *for* them and 'be their voice' so they will know what they mean and to say when ready. This helps to develop their internal language, even if they don't express it in any way.

Showing refers to anything you do that is visual that helps your child understand what you are saying. This could mean pointing, making a big gesture, or showing a picture for example.

Children often focus on intriguing and exciting things and usually like it when things go wrong or need fixing. You can add big gestures by noticeably moving your arms and using an excited voice with interesting tones and 'sound effects' (see Strategy 7).

To help share joint interest with your child, you can point to what they are already looking at. That way, your child doesn't need to shift their attention to something else. This makes it easier for them. It can be a neat, pressure-free way to support your child's developing joint attention skills.

So, if you spot your child looking out the window, go over to them and figure out what they might be looking at. Then point and comment: if they are looking at the branches of trees moving in the wind, you could point and say, '*Look! It's so windy! Woooooosh!*'. (Big gesture plus sound effect). Then pause for a few seconds for your child to process what you have said. They might make a sound back, although we are not waiting for or expecting them to do so. Whether they respond or not, you could point again (to whatever they are already looking at) and make another relevant comment after several seconds. Leave enough pause for them to process your words and potentially communicate something. We will talk in more detail later about what you can say and how you can say it.

4. GIVE IT (IF POSSIBLE)

One frequent reason that children communicate, either with or without words, is to ask for something. They might ask for food, a toy or another object or a fun activity they want. If you realize that your child communicated to ask for something physically, or by making a sound, or saying a word or words, and it is something that you can give them, then accept their first attempt and give it to them right away. Don't wait for them to say or ask again because they have already communicated it, and you have already understood!

For example, if your child likes a particular book about a bus, and reaches up to the shelf and starts to try to say 'beep beep' sounds or hums the bus song, then you could give that book to them right away after you have listened and acknowledged (*'okay! Yes!'* while smiling and nodding), and modeled and shown (pointing and saying, *'The bus book!.... Let's get it!.... I love this one!'*).

YES AND NO

Please note that when we refer to 'never denying' and always giving your child what they want when they have communicated something, you must prioritize your child's safety and honor your parenting boundaries. For example, what if they want to sit on the open oven door? It is clearly unsafe. What if they would like cookies at bedtime? This may break your parenting boundaries. Life gets in the way sometimes, too. You might be rushing out for an appointment, and playing the game your child wants at that moment may not be possible.

Sometimes, we can avoid saying 'no' by saying something like 'not right now!' or 'later!' and gently distracting them with another toy or activity they really enjoy. Then, ensure you fulfill your promise that they can have it or do it later. This approach can avoid some meltdowns.

But if your child persists, you may need to set a clear boundary with a strong 'no'. Make sure your body language matches your message: look firm (not angry) as you say 'no'. Shake your head and add a clear hand gesture as you say it, for example, swiping your hand diagonally downward, from your left shoulder towards your right hip, for example.

Once we have said 'no', we must stick to it; we cannot change our minds and go back on what we said. Your child needs you to be true to your word so they learn to understand and trust what your words mean to build trust in you.

We know that children develop an understanding of 'no' first. But equally, when your child is allowed something, make a point of saying 'yes' along with clear head nods so that they can learn the meaning of both 'yes' and 'no'. Again, we must honor our 'yes' once we have said it; we cannot go back on it.

So always *pause and give yourself time* to think before you answer with either a 'yes' or a 'no' so that you will provide an answer you can stick with. This will help your child understand the language of clear boundaries, which is so important for children to feel secure.

BIG GESTURES

Big gestures can be anything that involves you moving your body or arms in a way that catches your child's gaze – in a natural way! As grownups, we often use our hands alongside our speech when communicating. We do this, especially when we are talking about things that we want to emphasize. For example, when the dog chewed a favorite book, we might raise our hands in desperation! Or when you win a game of charades, you might punch the air in excitement. Similarly, big gestures can help make what you say seem important to your child. It can help them to notice you, look at you for longer, engage with you, and understand your message more.

One example is of a young girl who liked to rip up newspapers for long periods on her own. She loved it when her mom sat in front of her and copied her. The girl started noticing and watching her mom more; she engaged more and for longer periods as a result of her mom using exaggerated big gestures while ripping newspapers.

Another example could be when Teddy goes missing, shrug as you say, *'Where's Teddy gone? I don't know!'*. Then you can use a big gesture to put out your hand for them to take it and say, *'Let's go find him!'*.

If your child is busy picking up jigsaw pieces and looking at them, you can sit opposite them and offer them pieces by using big gestures or clear arm movements to catch their eye. It's okay if your child doesn't look in your direction; we are simply trying to find ways to encourage fun connection with you. If they are not in the mood, then we must respect that too. Big gestures, making your voice sound interesting, and using 'sound effects' are all strategies to help you get in touch with your own enthusiasm. And if you are more enthusiastic, this will send your child a message that whatever you are doing is fun! This can create more opportunities for connection with you.

The main goal of big gestures is to encourage your child to notice you more so there is more opportunity for connection between you. If you exaggerate your movements and make everything seem fun, your child will likely realize it is a fun game! You can adjust the style or speed of your big gestures depending on your child's mood. Don't feel like your child has to ask for each puzzle piece; it's okay to carry on your own 'solo goes' and keep handing a few pieces without expectation, using your big gestures! This can be a handy tip if your child starts to lose interest, and it might help them stay engaged and have fun with you for a little longer. But if your child is enjoying the game and looking to you for the next one, this means they are anticipating the next step! And if you are occasionally late with offering the next piece, they might ask for one in a different way.

IMPORTANT: Bear in mind that some children prefer less visual distraction and calm voices, so match your gestures and level of animation to what suits your child best. Not all children enjoy when others use big gestures or loud expressive voices, but you may already have noticed this if this applies to your child. If this is the case, gently vary the size, speed or frequency of your movements and sound of your voice. Find out what your child likes best by watching how they respond. Keep this in mind during our next video challenge. If this applies to you and your child, you may need to tone down your movements and your volume rather than increasing them.

'BIG GESTURES' VIDEO CHALLENGE

Record yourself interacting with your child for two to three minutes. During that time, try to vary how you use your arms when you talk, to help your child to notice you more. Here are some examples: if you are playing with bubbles, talk about how big it was and add a big gesture, or if you are playing with cars, talk about *'beep beep!'* or *'Let's drive!'* and add a big point or driving gesture to go with your words. Keep adding a big gesture that is linked to anything that you say.

Now watch your video back:

1. What difference, if any, did adding big gestures make to your interaction with your child?
2. Did they notice you more?
3. Did they have fun and engage with you more easily?
4. Did they start getting animated, too?
5. Did you find they didn't like the big gestures or animation in your voice or face? If so, what worked best for them?
6. Write down what works best for your child and let others who communicate with your child know so they can do it too.

You can note your thoughts here:

'LIFT MY VOICE'

As adults, we often speak in a low register with our own voice. Some of us naturally speak quietly, some of us talk fast, and some of us slowly. It would be very boring if we all sounded the same!

Most babies and young children tend to focus on higher-frequency sounds. It stands to reason that when we lift our voice up a few notes, it really catches a child's attention. It assists them to notice and engage with us more and ultimately focus more on our spoken language.

It can be difficult to change the way we speak. In effect, it's the equivalent of asking someone who is not Scottish to talk in a Scottish accent and to remember to do it for the whole day! Speaking in a new way may take a little practice.

IMPORTANT: This strategy is beneficial for most children. But for some children, higher or louder voices may be difficult to tolerate, and they may respond better to lower calmer voices. I remember one boy who used to get up and walk away from his mom when she tried to join him to play with him. We wondered if it was because she had a naturally loud, fast voice. When she experimented with her voice, she found that when she said less and spoke slowly and calmly, he tolerated her joining him and started to connect with her. You can gently experiment with your voice by going higher or lower, louder or softer. Find out what your child likes best by watching how they respond. Keep this in mind during our next video challenge if you think this applies to you and your child.

'LIFT MY VOICE' QUICK CHALLENGE

Do this quick practice now:

1. Use your normal voice to say out loud, '*This is so cool.*'
2. Now say '*Aaaaaaah!*' in your normal speaking voice and hold it for as long as possible. As you say '*Aaaaaaah!*' try slowly raising your voice like a sliding scale, as if you were singing and want to glide up to reach higher notes.
3. Find a spot that still feels natural and comfortable for you and repeat the phrase: '*This is so cooool!*' using those higher notes you just found.

Now consider these questions:

- Knowing your child, which way might sound more interesting to your child?
- To which way would your child be more likely to respond?
- If your child responds well to the higher or new tone, could you bring it into your everyday communication with your child in a way that still sounds natural?
- What kinds of things could you say?
- List a few fun sounds or comments you will try to use with your higher voice.
- After a few days, write down the impact of your new tone on your child's ability to connect with you.
- Some examples of things to say could be '*Wow!*' '*That's right!*' '*Let's do it!*' '*All done!*'. Instant enthusiasm!

- Conversely, if your child responds better to calmer lower tones, you may need to practice slowing down and speaking more quietly. Find a happy balance that suits your child.

When you experiment with your tone, alternating higher and lower tones as you speak, it brings your words to life. When you do this, it also really helps your child to process what you are saying. It can be challenging if your natural tone is soft or doesn't tend to vary or if you have a very fast rate of speech and find it hard to slow down. But you can practice, and it does become easier the more you do it. Don't worry if you try and try but find this strategy too challenging. For some individuals, it can be extremely difficult to change how we speak. I suggest this as a tool for your toolbelt because it can be so effective for children who struggle to tune into other's speech. But there are plenty of other useful strategies if this is challenging for you.

The reason we focus on 'Big Gestures' and 'Lift My Voice' in this chapter is because this is what works best for *most* children. But as we have mentioned, there are some children for whom this combination does not work. So, experiment and find out what works best for your child. When you combine 'Big Gestures' and 'Lift my Voice' strategies, it can really have a huge effect on how your child interacts with you - once you find the right natural combination that they enjoy.

For those of you who have a child who enjoys big gestures and animated tones, it can be tricky to balance sounding natural while using big gestures and an excited tone of voice - all simultaneously. Keep practicing the strategies together in your Video Challenges from now on, and in time, it should become second nature. If you need a reminder, think 'children's entertainer'! This often helps parents remember what we mean when we talk about big gestures and an interesting tone of voice.

For those of you who have a child who prefers calmer or low bassy voices, and if you are naturally animated, it can be tricky to balance slowing down your speech, using softer tones, or pulling back on your body movements when any one of these don't come naturally to you. Again, practice for a few minutes a day. Don't feel under pressure to change everything all at once. You can focus on one aspect at a time, for example, slowing down your speech while remaining natural-sounding. You will get a feel for what works for both you and your child over time.

'RESPOND WITH ENTHUSIASM' QUICK CHALLENGES:

1. Listen, Acknowledge, Model and Show, and Give (Where Possible):

- Write down the four-point plan in a thick pen on a sticky: 'Listen, Acknowledge, Model and Show, Give (where possible)'.
- Write 'Big Gestures' and 'Lift My Voice' (or whatever combination works best for your child) on another sticky.
- Put the stickies on the wall or the fridge somewhere your child usually requests or connects with you to communicate.
- Remember to glance over regularly throughout the day when your child is trying to connect or communicate with you so you remember what to do.

2. Practice saying 'no' out loud right now as you read this, with a firm voice and neutral face (neither smiling nor angry). Add a clear hand gesture swiping downwards and shake your head once, doing

all these gestures together as you say the word 'no'. How did that feel? Do you think your child will be more likely to learn the meaning of 'no' if you say it the same way each time?

3. Now practice saying 'yes' out loud with an upbeat tone, an open, smiling face, and a clear head nod. How did that feel?

- Do you usually emphasize 'no' and don't focus so much on highlighting 'Yes' with your child?
- How could you include more opportunities to highlight 'Yes' to your child so they can understand what it means?
- You could start by noticing when your child wants something so you can respond and answer '*Yes!*' for them. For example, when they go over to where the crackers are kept, you could say something like: '*Oh! Crackers? YES! (big nods and smile) Let's get some crackers!*'.
- Try to imagine yourself in a scenario where your child usually wants something.
- Could you say what it is ('Oh! Crackers?') and then say 'Yes!' with a clear but natural head nod?

4. Make a note for yourself with the words 'yes' and 'no' in a thick dark pen on a yellow sticky to put on the wall to help you remember to send your child clear yes / no messages from now on.

WIRED FOR COMMUNICATION: TWO POSSIBLE WAYS

Children process language or meaning differently by focusing on different aspects of what they hear.

When we think about how children learn, we usually expect children to learn to understand and use single words first. Then, when they use a variety of single words, we expect them to combine them into short phrases like, '*More brekkie!*' or '*teddy fall!*'. But there is another way that children can focus on meaning: through the intonation or the 'music' of the spoken voice. When we as adults speak in phrases and sentences, there is a cadence, rhythm, and a lift and fall in our voices as we talk. It makes our voices sound dynamic, in the same way that music does when we hear a musical phrase being sung - it's the same principle. The focus is the longer 'string', not a single unit like a word or a note.

This other way of learning language is often overlooked but can be a key component for some children to learn meaning, especially early on, before they learn what individual words mean and how they work. During this time, children rely on the music of the voice and the way that we speak to interpret our emotions and what is going on around them. They may become familiar with certain 'strings' or phrases without actually understanding what each word means, as in the example: '*We're all done!*' or '*Time to say night night!*'. You may find your child responding to these phrases when they are in context first, before they understand what individual words are: they are focusing on the string and your 'intonation' or the music in your voice.

All children spend time learning meaning in this way. Often, once children recognize that the strings are composed of individual 'units' or words, they will switch to focusing on individual words, and then we see them learning to use a variety of words and phrases in the way most people expect. We call these language users 'Analytic Language Processors' (ALP). They gradually construct longer and longer, more complex novel phrases spontaneously.

Some children show a preference for focusing on 'strings' of sounds and the music of the voice for much longer. They can become very adept at memorizing strings like numbers, letters or phrases and may use them to communicate with others. Sometimes, this sounds like well-formed phrases that they have picked up from others around them or from favorite clips they like to watch from entertainment media, like 'Uh oh spaghettios!' for example. Sometimes, children 'chatter' in a conversational way without well-formed words, so it sounds like lots of unintelligible strings of sound. We call these language learners' Gestalt Language Processors' (GLP).

It is important to mention that not all children who are unintelligible are automatically GLPs though, as there could be other reasons for the chatter: for example, it could be difficult for them to produce certain speech sounds, which could make their attempts sound like unintelligible chatter. A speech therapist familiar with both speech challenges and a GLP approach can advise you on this.

We must gain an understanding as to how a child is currently processing meaning because this can influence how we help them learn language. We want to give them what they need, in *their* way; the way that suits *them* best. We want to make the most of their amazing language-learning strengths.

Some children can process meaning in both ways simultaneously: even we as adults use terms like 'spill the beans' - we are not actually processing the word 'beans' and 'spilling' them! We process the whole phrase to mean that someone has said something that perhaps they shouldn't! We enjoy processing music as a 'whole' event, too, just like our children. Some of us like to add movie quotes into regular conversation because it's fun or because the situation exactly matches it: 'You're going to need a bigger boat!'. Some of us (like myself!) don't focus so much on the words in the song, but remember the melodies well. But as adults, we have also learned to process and interpret the meaning of individual words.

So we can use a combination of both ways to communicate with each other.

Remember also that regardless of whether your child is an ALP, a GLP, or a combination of both, a 'Dual Language Processor' (DLP), they already have some internal language. There are aspects to your voice they focus on and recognize, even if they are not saying words, sounds, or phrases yet. They could focus on your tone of voice, the rhythm of your words, and how your voice sounds musical when it goes up and down as you speak. These all have meaning and represent language for them. So, it can be misleading to talk about children being 'non-verbal' because all children have some internal language and draw meaning from what they hear. The terms' non-speaking or 'minimally speaking' are more accurate.

Of course, none of us have a crystal ball: we don't know how far along the language learning process children will go. This depends on their own ability level. Our best approach is to meet them where they are at. By doing this, we give them the best chance to reach their full potential. Like everything in this book, that likely means adapting what *we* are doing, not because what we did before was wrong but because some strategies work better for some children than others.

Let's explore Analytic and Gestalt Language Processing in more detail in the next section.

Analytic Language Processors (ALPs)

The analytic way is one way to learn meaning. It describes how some children show an interest in learning word labels first (*'bottle', 'bubbles'*), then combe words into flexible combinations (*'mommy bottle', 'big bubble'*) that gradually increase in length and complexity until finally, they produce self-generated grammatically correct sentences (*'Where's the bottle mommy?', 'I wanna bigger bubble!'*). This is the expectation that most parents have when they think of the path their child will take when learning to communicate.

In summary, ALPs usually start with a single word as the basic unit of meaning. Then they start combining more and more words together in new ways until they are producing self-generated phrases and sentences.

Gestalt Language Processors (GLPs)

Much of the literature on GLPs comes from observing children's chatter. Sometimes, this 'chatter' can seem meaningless. You may read this in formal medical or speech therapy books as 'echolalia' or 'delayed echolalia'. These terms have a negative association - but nothing could be further from the truth! This is a very valid way of processing meaning and using it to communicate something.

The kind of chatter we are talking about happens when a child repeats what others say word-for-word but much later on. It is easy to know where the child has 'lifted' the words or phrases from if their words are clear, but chatter can also consist of rich musical tones in the voice that sounds like conversation but without any clear words, or maybe just one word here or there. When a pattern of musical tones in chatter is recognizably repeated, it is likely it has meaning for that person.

These strings of sound, whether clear or unclear, are all considered to be distinct 'scripts' that they have heard somewhere. Or, more accurately, we call these longer strings 'Gestalts'.

Gestalts usually have meaning for the child and communicate something. So we can take it that most strings or 'chatter' have meaning for the child, whether we are privy to it or not! We may never know.

Sometimes, though, children (and grownups!) like to repeat particular sounds or phrases to themselves. For some, it helps them self-regulate: to stay happy and calm. My son used to hum while he drew or busied himself because he liked it, and it made the experience more fun for him. But even when a child is repeating favorite sounds, words, or phrases to self-regulate, it still communicates something to us - that they enjoy this activity and that it is likely helping them to stay happy and calm.

Many GLPs store a set of distinct Gestalts that have a unique meaning for them. Their vocabulary can look different because it consists of separate long strings as their units of meaning. For some, these Gestalts may be long strings of clear language. For others, Gestalts may consist of unclear chatter or sounds with no clear words, mimicking the sound of conversation. Some children's Gestalts are interesting musical sounds like a hum or a vowel sound that might raise or fall, mimicking an exclamation they may have heard someone say previously like *'Don't worry!'* but without the actual consonants or speech sounds. Or *'Uh oh!'* is often a Gestalt that could be used to convey that something untoward has happened!

We all use Gestalts. For example, when we say *'nooks and crannies',* *'safe and sound',* or when we remember lyrics of songs or quote movie scripts. These are all Gestalts that we store as whole units. We don't wonder what a 'cranny' is when we say 'nooks and crannies'! It's more about the whole concept of tiny little places.

While Analytic Language Processors learn from the ground up (from single words to complex strings or sentences), Gestalt Language Processors learn from the top down: They start with the longer strings. The journey to self-generated new phrases and sentences can be a long one, but at least now we have signposts to follow.

Until recently, most of the speech therapy supports we used were based on the Analytic way of processing language. Working with Gestalt Language Processing is new for many of us, and some therapists have yet to hear or learn about it.

In recent years, Marge Blanc developed a framework to help assess and support individuals suspected of leaning towards a Gestalt Language Processing way of identifying meaning. Her framework offers one system for speech therapists to follow with a clear structure for supporting GLPs through their language learning path. This approach makes it a lot easier to support communication development of those who show strengths in processing strings of information, especially when children start to use strings of words.

Marge Blanc's 'Natural Language Acquisition' framework describes how some GLPs grow their repertoire with various strings or phrases that have meaning for them. ('Oh no!', 'That's all, folks!' 'Up, up and away!' 'Time *to go*!') Once they have a range of different Gestalts, some GLPs start to spot similarities in the chunks of different Gestalts ('*We need* + some juice', *We need* + another one', 'Time + *to go*', 'Mom has + *to go*'). Then GLPs work out how to isolate these smaller chunks of language and recombine or mix and match them with other chunks (*We need* + *to go*!'). Eventually, they chunk down to isolate individual word meanings ('*We* + *go*').

So their process consists of gradually figuring out the code and how to break down their longer Gestalts into smaller parts until they eventually identify single words. Once they crack the code, GLPs are in a position to start building up their sentences from single words into new spontaneous self-generated phrases and sentences, eventually with grammar, just like the ALP. For those GLPs who acquire spoken language, their journey can take longer to get there, but the end goal is the same: novel, spontaneous, self-generated language.

To recap, instead of their basic unit being a single word, a GLP's basic starting unit consists of long strings of sounds like babble or chatter, humming melodies from songs, excerpts of books they connect with, quotes from video clips they like or exact repetitions of what they have previously heard others around them saying. The speech can be clear and adult-like or like unclear conversational 'chatter'. It is important to remember that these Gestalts usually have meaning for the child, and the meaning may not always be obvious to others.

Some Gestalt Language Processors enjoy the alphabet or numbers because they follow a neat sequence or string that can be repeated. Once they learn a spoken string, it can feel familiar, safe, and fun. Some GLPs even repeat whole sequences from books clearly or may repeat entire favorite parts of episodes from their favorite shows. This repetition can be their main form of communication. Parents can be confused when they hear their little one repeating many sentences word for word but are not carrying on to-and-fro interaction or conversation with them in natural everyday situations. This is because the GLP's path to learning language can look very different from the ALP's path. The sounds, humming, unintelligible chatter, or phrase repetitions are their path to language acquisition but can seem irrelevant to many of us. Unless we realize the importance of their sounds, hums, and chatter, we can often ignore these golden nuggets of communication.

So far, for those of us familiar with the GLP approach, we are currently guided by information from individual case studies and by therapist experience (including my own). But the hope is that more robust studies will soon add to our evidence base. In the meantime, we will continue to feel our way based on our own clinical observations and on useful supports like Marge Blanc's 'Natural Language Acquisition' framework.

Many clinicians and parents tell us that Marge Blanc's 'Natural Language Acquisition' framework is working for them, helping some children develop their communication skills in a natural and fun child-led way. Remember that this approach seems to work best for children who show an interest in using communication consisting of longer strings of information like songs, or language stored in chunks, or who are already using words in long strings that have been 'lifted' from somewhere and repeated word for word.

You can take the information in this book and make your own informed choice based on what you observe works for your child. Some of our strategies are designed specifically with the Gestalt Language Processor in mind - those children who focus on longer strings of language and the musicality of the spoken voice. This can be especially relevant for children who have not used their first clear words but may use their voice with emotion to tell you what they want. It is what some people think of as meaningless 'chatter', but I think of it as an amazing way to communicate wants or seek comfort.

There is also a benefit in applying some of the general GLP strategies and guidelines to *all* young children. This is because we believe all young children go through a Gestalt phase of language processing where they tune into the 'sing-song' nature of what we say. For example, most children go through a phase of understanding or saying *'All done!'* or *'All gone!'* as whole units. Another way that some children acquire or use a Gestalt is to over-apply a single word or words in many situations: for example, using the word '*Cat*' to apply to any four-legged animal. Many children will do this before they start to learn the distinction between different labels and types of animals.

These are features of Gestalt Language Processing and apply to all language learners at one time or another. So, the way we model language for GLPs using natural conversational 'kidspeak' and *child-led play-based* therapy is highly recommended.

There is much evidence already for the benefits of child-led play and modeling language structures in short phrases for very young children so they can hear how language and conversation work naturally and in everyday situations (rather than in situations led and prompted by adults).

We have already talked about some GLP characteristics. Let's explore how those who would benefit from a Gestalt approach may present in more detail next.

Imagine only connecting with the topics or events that appeal to you. When you experience that exciting event or topic, it triggers extreme emotion in you - be that excitement, joy, wonder. All your senses are heightened; the sounds, smells, joy, language, and physical and emotional feelings are all bundled up together. You may not even be able to extract which bit of you is feeling what because the experience is all rolled up into one whole experience, like a ball of string you can't unknot. It is all stored together in your memory as a 'whole' complete unit. So, each time you think of or experience that fun thing, that ball of emotion and experience is triggered for you and brings up that extreme experience in your mind.

An example to illustrate this is when you go on a roller coaster. The physical and emotional feelings you go through are extreme! And you may lose track of what's happening around you - this is a 'ball of string' moment. You can probably recall the fun and excitement (or stress!) when you think of a ride on a rollercoaster.

For some individuals, that extreme 'ball of string' experience can happen for what others might consider mundane things, like when things are in a neat line, or if a puzzle is completed, from moving their hands or body in a particular way, or from the feeling of running or crashing on the cushions of the sofa. Those who are using language may feel that hit of emotion from talking about their favorite topic and could talk about it all day long!

But when you experience that kind of extreme joy from your favorite activities or events, then anything that you don't connect with just seems like 'background noise'. It doesn't give you the impact of that ball of experience and emotion, so you don't pay much attention to it because it feels so humdrum. It is a bit like when we go to a bad movie or a long, boring webinar; we lose attention or switch off completely. We might even walk away or walk out of the movie theatre because it might be really hard to stay and watch a movie that is so uninteresting.

But for those individuals we are talking about, the usual humdrum could be things that you and I might consider interesting: playing with certain fun toys, playing in a certain way, listening to someone talking about anything that isn't their favorite thing, basically anything that doesn't give that 'ball of string' feeling of excitement or satisfaction.

So, some children may show a preference for playing in a certain way and might not like it when we try to change it. It is tantamount to someone saying to us, 'Now you have to sleep on the other side of the bed that you normally do'. I know I would hate that. It would be so disorientating! I probably wouldn't sleep very well, and I would try everything to get to sleep on my preferred side of the bed.

When we understand this way of experiencing the world, it all starts to make sense. We have the key to unlocking connection with our child - in *their* way. A great first step is noticing those ball-of-string moments of joy. When we go with them and support our children to experience even more joy, this is the foundation for connecting with them. We can join in, even if it means just watching from a distance and adding language to that 'ball of string' moment. Then, the language will become part of their memorable experience of joy. This is one way we can add language to their world in the best possible way for them to connect with it.

The kinds of things that capture a GLP's interest will be individual. It may relate to their senses: if they have a preference for looking at objects in a close, intense way, then they seek visual joy. If they like toys that make sound or music, then they seek listening joy. If they seek out movement like running, climbing, or rough and tumble, then they seek movement joy. Or they may seek a combination of the senses to find their ball-of-string joy.

For example, when a toy falls unexpectedly, it might capture their interest. We interpret this by noticing changes in their facial expression, body language, and how they seem engaged or connected with what's happening. Then, when we add a musical-sounding exclamation like '*Uh ohhh!*' or '*Oh Noooo!*', this imprints like a 'sound effect' associated with that intriguing context or situation. We are adding to the ball of string moment.

The next time something falls, that memory may get triggered for the GLP and prompt them to remember or say, '*Uh Ohhh!*' or '*Oh Noooo!*'. Even without clear speech, they might say something using the same tone of voice that they heard for '*Uh Oh!*' or '*Oh Noooo!*'. Even if they don't say anything, they may replay the memory inside their mind. We may not know when this is happening, but it demonstrates another reason why we need to pause a lot: so that they have time to process or replay their stored memories and make these important connections. This is their way of learning, so we must honor that.

When you listen to your child (Strategy 3), make sure to tune into their little sounds and chatter that you might normally tune out of. Listen to their conversation-like sounds. Do you notice any patterns of intonation in their voice that mimic what other people say but without words? Can you pinpoint what it is and where it comes from? Is it a snippet from their favorite character or video clip they like to watch? Or is it from something that you often say? '*Wow!*' is one of the little sayings that I'm told I often repeat! I never realized this until someone pointed it out to me. I always wondered why some children often said *'Wow!'* around me.

Here is an example of a child who leaned towards a Gestalt way of processing language: He associated the phrase 'go outside' with feeling happy because when going outside, which he really loves, his parents say, '*Let's go outside!*'. He may repeat this phrase '*go outside*' later on, even when he is back inside, cozy and warm, when he has no further intentions of going outside again. Why might he do this? We guessed that he learned to associate that phrase with feeling happy. So that might be the closest 'Gestalt' he has to represent his feelings at that moment: *'happy'*. This was his ball-of-string moment. He may also use that phrase to help himself self-regulate or self-soothe if feeling anxious, for example. Either way, the phrase communicates something, and it's up to us to do the work to figure out what that might be, if we can.

Remember that all children will go through a phase of this kind of 'whole unit' processing, just like we mentioned that '*All done!*' or '*All gone!*' are phrases with more than one word but are first learned as a whole unit by young children, and are associated with the idea of there being nothing left.

When learning language, some children use this whole unit Gestalt way of processing language for a little while, then quickly break down the phrases and move to single-word processing. So if we use our example of 'all gone', they learn that 'all' means *everything* and 'gone' means *not here.*

They may still use some learned phrases, so they can appear to be mixed or a Dual Language Processor (DLP), using a combination of both Gestalt and Analytic ways of processing language; a combination of learned 'whole' phrases but also combining single words into new phrases creatively by themselves.

But for others, the Gestalt 'whole unit' way of storing whole phrases and sentences may remain their preferred way of processing. We aim to support the GLP's way of learning language in this 'whole phrase' way. Ideally, we want every child to be able to express themselves in a way that others can understand, by whatever means. So when we start by helping them develop in the way their brain is set up to do, we are helping them to reach their full potential. We can really support their language learning journey by giving them the language in the way their brain needs it.

So once we have identified a child is learning meaning and processing in this 'whole unit' way, it has implications for how we help support their language learning journey; we will see some examples of how to do this shortly.

When a true Gestalt Language Processor is using speech, they may use their lifted whole phrases or Gestalts at times that do not seem to us to connect with what's happening. But it very likely has meaning for them!

A GLP may do this because they may use the most natural string for them or the only string at their disposal, particularly if they have an urgent need. An example of this is a child who might say,

'Don't worry! Mommy's coming' even when their mom is right there in front of them. The phrase might be lifted from what their mom usually says when something is amiss. The 'ball of string' moment means that this was the phrase the child chose to say because it was all tied up with the experience of something being amiss.

This communication method may not fit the 'conventional' language learning rules we have historically come to know or expect. We need to meet Gestalt Language Processors where they are: We need to become a 'Sound Detective' to work out what their unclear chatter might mean, or a 'Phrase Detective' if they have clear phrases. We need to figure out the hidden meaning for our child. It may not be what it first appears to be! But when you observe a Gestalt Language Processor's experiences and know them well, you may start to piece together patterns when they make certain sounds or say certain phrases. Once you trace their lifted phrases back to the source, it can give you clues as to what meaning your child may have associated with that lifted phrase. For example, if your child saw a cartoon clip of a big scary dog and a character placating the dog by saying *'There there, good doggie!'* - if this was a scary 'ball of string' moment for your child, maybe 'There there, good doggie!' is what they might say in another situation when they feel scared.

Consider another example of a child who loves a favorite storybook about a monster. One day, on a Winter walk with his mom, he kept repeating *'had no whiskers'* from the storybook. His mom had no idea what this was about because it had no obvious connection to the walk. There were no animals around; it was a windy Winter's day. When she got home and settled down to look at his favorite storybook with him, she noticed a part of the story mentioned *'whiskers'*. The page had a picture set in a snowy Winter scene.... She realized that her child had associated the phrase about the 'whiskers' with the concept of being cold! They had been cold on the walk because it was windy. She had to be a phrase detective, and she figured out his message: He had been trying to tell her that he was cold.

We may often ignore these longer strings of sounds, chatter, or words, but they have immense value to you if your most natural way to organize the world is through longer strings of information. Those strings are your communication currency. But it takes someone to really tune in to you and respond for these messages to be received and validated.

Only someone who knows your child well is in a position to be a sound or phrase detective. You, as a parent, will be in the best place to understand what your child has been exposed to and what possible meaning it may have for them when you really tune in. Teachers may also have valuable insight into what they have been exposed to. It is important to join the dots with input from everyone who knows a GLP to spot patterns, trace the sources of their sounds or phrases, and figure out what hidden messages they could be communicating. These give us clues on how to respond and the type of language to model back to them.

How do we help their communication to develop? We support their exploration of language and communication through child-led play. This means playing what *they* want to play, even if this is not the usual play we expect: maybe they like spinning lids or lining up objects on a (cold) radiator. These could be their 'ball of string' moments of joy. We also need to model possible Gestalts in the most natural way for them, alongside what they are experiencing, so they can tune into the language we offer. We don't force language, ever. We don't sit down at a table and do 'work' to show them how phrases can be broken up - they do that all by themselves within their own head, and at their own speed. Our role is to support their process: We bring language options on a virtual 'tray' by modeling natural phrases that seem like a good fit for what they might be thinking or sensing at that moment, using *their* voice as if we are their mouthpiece. 'It's so crunchy!' 'I like this one!' 'No way!' 'Let's play, Mommy!'.

When offered many phrases over time at the right level for them to understand and connect with, they may eventually break down the chunks bit by bit and identify and isolate single words. If a child is at this point, they understand that words can operate entirely independently and be recombined together into brand-new self-generated phrases. This whole process does not happen overnight and can take months or years. We cannot determine the length of their path or the end point of a child's communication learning journey. This will depend on a child's own individual ability level. Some will continue with their preferred Gestalt way of communicating or self-soothing by using their favorite sounds, chatter, songs or phrases.

Even if an individual learns how to break down language into units and recombine them into self-generated sentences, longer strings may always be the natural 'go-to' for some individuals, which is okay! In the same way we use movie quotes or sayings in our own chat, like 'Houston, we have a problem!' or 'Here's looking at you, kid!'.

In my opinion, it would not make sense *not* to offer the option of Gestalt Language support so that an individual can reach their best level of self-agency. We have an obligation to assist individuals in reaching their communication potential, avoiding misunderstandings, and expressing themselves successfully with others who may not know how to interpret those longer strings of language. Especially if getting there involves no extra 'work' on the part of the child's and is geared towards generating fun and joyful moments for them!

We will not be going into detail about how to help children who are already using long phrases in this book. Here, we discuss practical early strategies for non-speakers and minimally speaking children. If your child is using long strings of lifted language or if you suspect your child might lean towards a Gestalt way of Language Processing, support is best led by a Speech Therapist familiar with GLP approaches. If your child is already talking using phrase or sentence Gestalts or scripts, you may seek out Marge Blanc's book (2012), "Natural Language Acquisition: The Journey from Echolalia to Self-Generated Language," and you can also check out www.meaningfulspeech.com for a useful blog and various informative courses.

Now you may be thinking: How can we work out if a child might benefit from either an Analytic or Gestalt approach, even before we hear them using words?

It can be challenging to tell if non-speakers or minimally speaking children will lean towards Gestalt or Analytic Language Processing. But some clues can help us. This will inform us about how to help them best, as the way we tap into GLPs' and ALPs' strengths is slightly different.

We believe that some Gestalt Language Processors may have an overall Gestalt way of learning. This can give clues to help us identify if a GLP approach will help them.

If several of these next points resonate with you, then your child might already be focusing on language in a GLP way:

1. GLPs often love music, even more so than expected. They may be able to sing or hum quite complex tunes even if they cannot use words yet.

2. GLPs can enjoy humming, singing, and using sound effects like *'Wow!', 'Uh Oh!'*, or little squeals and other random noises.
3. GLPs might inconsistently join in for the *'go'* in *'Ready steady...GO!'* and may not use it outside of one particular situation, or else may overuse it.
4. Some GLPs might say something on one occasion out of the blue that really surprises you and then may never say it again. One recent example is of a minimally speaking child who said 'g'luck' (good luck) to a departing family relative once, then never said it again. 'Good luck' is what the family relative usually says when leaving.
5. Some Gestalt learners like completion, for example, fully closing the train track circle or putting all the puzzle pieces away before they can move on to something else.
6. Some Gestalt learners like to play their own way, make a pattern, or do things in a certain sequence. Often, the sequence is how they have chosen to do it, and they may like to do it that way every time or most times.
7. Some Gestalt learners like to watch certain parts of video clips over and over again and may act them out. You may notice them trying to enact parts of the dialogue, even without words. They might like to visit a particular page in a favorite book each time they pick it up and ignore the rest. Some Gestalt learners may copy certain physical gestures or movements that will have meaning for them, and they may echo these gestures later to convey meaning.
8. Some Gestalt learners show that they remember a place after having been there just once or recognize when you take a different route than usual in the car.
9. A percentage of Gestalt Language Processors are thought to be hyperlexic. For non-speakers and minimally speaking children, this means that they might be interested in letters or the alphabet from an early age and may like to

line up, point out, spell out, name letters they see, or even learn to read some words from a very early age, often before they can use language to communicate effectively.

10. Some GLPs quickly learn to do something new after seeing it done only once or sometimes without being shown how to at all! For example, a child may have a scooter and never show any interest in it. Then, one day, they pick it up by themselves and just know how to ride it, with no learning curve.

Some children have characteristics very clearly associated with either ALP or GLP characteristics. Some children lean more towards either one way or the other. But it's important to remember that it's not a hard and fast rule: some children can have ALP and GLP characteristics simultaneously. All children go through a GLP stage; some move into an ALP way of processing relatively quickly, and others remain in the GLP stages for much longer as their natural communication method.

The seven strategies in this book are designed to benefit both Analytic and Gestalt Language Processors in the early stages of communication development.

IMPORTANT: Analytic strategies tend not to work so well for Gestalt Language Processors. If unsure, follow the GLP strategies, which are useful for *both* Analytic and Gestalt processors.

Analytic Language Processor: What to Say and How to Say It

Analytic Language Processors are described as learning from the ground up; they like to learn individual word meanings first (*'Mommy!', 'Car!'*). They may look to you to name things for them and enjoy learning new words. They also learn new words every week and may generalize them easily and flexibly to new situations, so they understand that the 'out' in 'out the door' is the same as taking a toy 'out' of the box and putting the cat 'out'. After learning to use approximately 50 words, ALPs start combining them into short two-word phrases, like 'Mommy car!' or 'Mommy's car!'. An ALP's speech doesn't have to be clear. Once you notice that they are learning single words and starting to combine them flexibly, you can be pretty sure they are processing language as an ALP.

Two Goals

We need to cater to two possible goals for an ALP: one to help develop their *understanding* and another to develop their ability to use words *expressively*. For example, when playing with a pig coin game, you can model single words for them to copy when they are ready (*'Pig!', 'Oink!'*). But you could also say a longer phrase so they learn to understand how the words work together (*'Look! The coin goes in the pig!'*). You can work on both these goals simultaneously by alternating naturally between single words and phrases during your chat. Remember to keep your comments relevant to what your child is likely thinking (Strategy 1: Get Out Of My Own Head).

Expression

When encouraging a non-speaking or minimally speaking ALP's language expression, you can use single words, especially if they show an interest in learning the names of different objects (*train*), actions (*jump*), or descriptions (*big*). It is important to point to what you are talking about or make the action simultaneously so they can pair your word with what they see so they can learn what your words mean. For example, when saying, 'Let's get a drink!' make a drinking gesture and point to the refrigerator.

We do not expect any child to copy us, and we never ask them to 'say it after me'. It is enough for them to hear you say a single word for them. If you are commenting on something they find fun, they will be more likely to want to join in themselves in whatever way they can. If they are not ready for words yet, you are showing them what they could say when they are ready.

For example, when building a tower of bricks, you could say *'Up up up!'* and point to the top of the tower, or 'another!' and point to one on the floor, or *'Higher!'* and make a big gesture when the tower gets really high. You could use a sound effect, 'Uh oh!' when the tower falls. All of these target something your child could say when ready.

Understanding

Ideally, with an Analytic Language Processor, we also want to promote language understanding by using short phrases up to 4-5 syllables long when speaking with your child. For example, when you want to draw attention to the brick falling off the top of the tower, you could say, *'Oh, look at the brick!'* and point to it. That phrase contains four syllables (excluding the 'Oh!'). Or you could say, *'It's gonna fall!'* which is another four-syllable phrase. Or when the bricks all fall, you can say the phrase *'Uh oh!... They all fell down!'*, a four-syllable phrase with an 'Uh oh!' sound effect.

ALPs need to hear short, clear phrases to develop their understanding of language. Phrases like *'Get your shoes!'* or *'Let's go out!'* benefit an ALP because they can hear how individual words fit into sentences and how they can be flexibly combined. An ALP's understanding of language is often (but not always) one step ahead of their ability to express themselves.

Anchor Words

Anchor words are words we repeat in several phrases when connecting with a child through play or when they show interest in something. We re-phrase what we say, keeping it relevant to what's happening, but we often retain one main 'anchor' word consistent in each phrase. This is so that we have many chances to model and demonstrate how that word works in different phrases and sentences. The aim is never for your child to repeat after you: We aim to let them hear and process what we say without expectation. We can leave pauses for them to process the words and to say something if they wish.

Here are some examples of how to use Anchor words with an Analytic Language Processor:

During play with a toy dinosaur, when a child is making the dinosaur eat off a plate, we could use the word 'dinosaur' as our anchor word:

- The dinosaur is hungry!
- Let's feed the dinosaur!
- Hey Dinosaur! Here's your plate!
- How about some cake for the dinosaur?

Depending on what's happening, we could use a different anchor word. For example, if a child's play is focused more on putting food items on the plate, we could say:

- Here's a plate
- Put some pizza on the plate!
- The plate's full!
- Dinosaur, do you want a plate?

Or if the play was focused on the dinosaur chasing others and making big roaring noises, we could say:

- Oh no! The dinosaur's gonna chase Monkey! Raaargh!
- Now Monkey's gonna chase him back!
- Who's he gonna chase now?
- Don't chase me, Dino!
- Go chase someone else!

When you use anchor words, try to match your phrase to the action as it happens. Don't say all your sentences back to back because your child won't have time to process them all. It is best to leave decent pauses of several seconds between each comment you make so your child has time to process your phrases. Your pauses will also leave space for your child to say something if they are ready to. If your child is not yet ready to say words, they might make a sound or take a turn by doing an action (*chasing Monkey*), looking at you, or showing you in some other way that they are listening. Make sure to stop talking for a longer time after you have used anchor words several times and see what your child does or says next. (Strategy 1: Get Out Of My Own Head).

If possible, aim for 4 or 5 phrases with your anchor word. But don't worry if you can't manage that many. The priority is to keep your chat conversational and relevant to what your child is interested in at that moment, so don't keep talking about boring plates if your child has moved on to fun chasing and roaring!

Do not use Anchor words with a Gestalt Language Processor. There are other strategies that better suit a GLP's way of processing, which we'll talk about next.

IMPORTANT: If your child is already using single words, don't assume your child is an Analytic Language Processor! We are primed as parents to 'teach' language in the Analytic way: we model single words as units *first.* Now imagine that you are a Gestalt Language Processor: if that's all that's on offer, you will 'record' single-word Gestalts with your fun, intriguing 'ball-of-string' experiences, and a single word is what you might say when a relevant feeling or experience is triggered in some way (*'Doggie!', 'want'* or *'more'*). This is language we have taught them, but it may not be aligned with their natural way of processing meaning. Many GLPs know the names of colors, numbers, names of favorite characters, and other lists. But what helps a GLP thrive is strings of longer words and phrases.... You can't break a single word down any more than to itself! So if we mostly focus on modeling single words to a GLP, then they learn those words as whole Gestalts and are missing what they need: longer phrases that they can break down into single words later if and when they are ready. They stay using single words because they haven't had the chance to hear the full phrases or strings to figure out how language works. If your child is using single words and is not experimenting by combining words together, then one of the reasons could be that they are a Gestalt Language Processor, and they need to hear natural melody and intonation in longer strings when you say longer conversational phrases.

Gestalt Language Processors: What to Say and How to Say It

For Gestalt Language Processors, we must be mindful that pointing to individual objects and naming them is not where we should ideally start. Instead, we need to tap into the GLP's strength: The GLP connects with longer strings and 'catchy' language, much like when we connect with the chorus of a catchy pop tune that 'hooks' us in and makes its way into our heads like an earworm. We need to provide earworms for our little GLPs so that they build up a bank of them over time: 'Let's go!' 'Put them on!' 'Look! It's sooooo funny!'. Those earworms must fit with what they are already thinking and enjoying. They are far less likely to connect with language we try to 'teach' them.

I need to mention our caveat again: not all children enjoy the sound of an animated voice with rich intonation. It depends on the child. But my experience is that 98% of children with sensory needs enjoy the melody and dynamic rising and falling intonation of a speaker. You will already have a good idea if your child doesn't respond well to animated voices or gestures, so observe your child's reactions and find out what kind of voice helps your child to be at their happiest and connect best with you.

You might notice similarities between the phrase models listed for ALPs and those listed for GLPs below. This is because we have real conversations with all our children, regardless of how they focus on language. But you may also notice a slight difference in the kinds of phrases we want to focus on specifically for the GLP.

For a GLP, conversational phrases are best. Why do we not specifically focus on teaching individual words, like nouns ('*doll/spoon*'), adjectives ('*hot/crunchy*'), or verbs ('*run/sleep*)? Because it likely won't resonate with our little GLPs! As we already mentioned, it may hold up their progress because they respond more naturally to catchy 'earworm' phrases. They need longer strings that ideally can be broken down into shorter chunks later on that can be mixed and matched when ready, like '*Let's go + outside! Let's go + to the park! Let's go + upstairs!*'. Remember, our goal is to support children to their best potential. In the case of a GLP, the end goal is for them to use self-generated language in whatever way helps them best and as far as their true potential leads them.

When you respond to your GLP, and if your child likes it when you're animated, remember to respond with enthusiasm! This is because they are more likely to process language delivered with emotion when it is connected with what they are thinking or experiencing at that moment. They will be more alert when something intriguing to them is happening or has just happened. This means noticing what grabs their interest using Strategy 1 and then using interesting intonation or interesting-sounding speech when you talk about what is fun about it, and ideally, what they are thinking or experiencing from their point of view (*'Oooooh! I like it! Wow! It's so fuzzy!', 'Oh no! It's falling down'!*). It also means making sure you are using 'sound effects' in your play with your child (see Strategy 7). But also make sure to comment using phrases because your little GLP may be more interested in the longer strings you say. (*'I love this one! No way! Take it out! It's so funny! I'm soooo tired!'*).

Avoid single words where possible in the early stages. It's not that single words are forbidden, but as we mentioned, putting your focus on teaching single words like the names of colors, vehicles, and animals will keep them learning single-word lists or scripts that cannot be further broken down.

Some children will enjoy naming letters, numbers and colors, and this is to be encouraged! Repeating them may be an activity they enjoy. But we can also feed their brain what it needs so they can figure out how language works and expand their communication experience. We can give them some useful, longer models: *'I like green', 'C comes next!', '10 is such a big number!'*. Some of these may 'stick' with your GLP and some won't, but that's okay! They will pick and choose whatever language strings work for them. Our focus is on modeling real conversational language without any expectation that they will do or say anything back. They do not need to say anything. We offer language, and they will pick up on what resonates for them and store them as Gestalts naturally, to be used later when they choose to.

Like with an ALP, we never ask a GLP to repeat or fill in a prompted phrase (It's a....?). We always model language without expectation.

So for the GLP, that means we model the whole phrase, so they get to hear how it is supposed to sound. We don't worry about breaking anything down - they can figure that out later on themselves as they go through their language-learning process at their own pace.

You'll notice the examples we have seen so far sound like 'kid-speak'! These are the conversational phrases that children say to each other. If you listen to children chatting together at a kid's party, are they teaching each other about the 'red truck' versus the 'green car'? No! There are bursts of busy conversation:

- That's mine!
- No, it's not!
- I like this one, can I have this one?
- It's a big one!
- Gimme it!

Did you notice any nouns, colors, or 'teachy' type words in these examples? No... that's not how kids speak to each other: they speak with drama and real intent. They send genuine messages and have meaningful things to say to each other conversationally.

So, when modeling language for a GLP, it is more efficient for language learning if we move our focus away from teaching individual word names. We don't need to focus specifically on naming things until they have a large repertoire of phrase-type strings and can already mix and match parts of phrases together flexibly to create new phrases and sentences.

At the moment, your job is to comment on your GLP's sensory and lived experience in a fun way, adding sound effects and excitement to their own personal movie, especially at times of high drama! (For those children who respond well to the dramatic way of playing).

Here are some examples of short 'sound effect' type Gestalts that you may already use and some longer ones that you can try to bring into the conversation:

Sound Effect Gestalts

- *Hey!* (For example, when a little brother comes over and grabs the brick your child wanted)
- *Wow!* (When you notice your child watching something super interesting happen)
- *No way!* (When something intriguing happens, for example, when two cars come down the car slide simultaneously).
- *Uh Oh!* (when something goes wrong)
- *Yay!* (When they succeed at something)
- *Whoooo!* or *Wheeee!* (When a car glides down the car slide)
- Shoo! Shoo! (When they are trying to 'shoo' away something)
- *Bzzzzz!* (When they take an interest in a bee or picture of a bee. Any animal sounds can be Gestalts if delivered in an interesting-sounding way that grabs your child.)

Phrase Gestalts

- *That's so cool! That's amazing*! (When you notice your child watching something super interesting happen)
- *Take it out*! (When they are taking their favorite stuffed toy out of the box)

- Let's put it in! (When pushing a shape into the shape sorter or a coin into the pig coin game - as an alternative to naming the shape or color.)
- *This is so much fun*! (When a toy rocket goes 'whoosh!' up into the sky!)
- *That's mine!* (For example, when a little brother comes over and grabs the brick your child wanted)
- *Not now, Mom*! (When they push you away)
- *I love this!* (When eating their favorite ice cream and really enjoying it!)
- *Let's do it again!* (Instead of 'Do you want to do it again?')
- *This is so chewy / crunchy / yummy!* (When they are chewing)
- *I love jumping!* (when they start jumping and really enjoy it)
- *I'm so tired... Time for bed!* (when you see them yawn at bedtime)
- *That looks nice! It's round / square*! (with toys, If you see that they like looking at a particular part of a toy or picture that has those attributes.)
- *It goes round and round and round*! (when there is a moving part they like to watch turn around.)
- *Oh, that's so fluffy / rough / smooth!* (when you see your child feeling something)
- *Bang bang bang! / Oh, that's noisy! / I like banging!* (If you see your child banging a toy, spoon, or bowl on the table.)
- *Beep beep! Coming through! Out of my way!* (When you see them rolling a car along.)
- *Look at that big dog!* (When you see a dog out walking)

Did you notice that many of the comments or Gestalt examples above are not specific to any play activity but to real-life situations? This is how a GLP will best learn to understand and communicate.

These types of comments may also look obvious now as you are reading them, but many of us don't realize that our 'default' position is either to ask questions or to comment on what things are called:

- What's this?
- What color is it?
- Where does it go?
- Do you want a drink?
- It's nice, isn't it?
- 'Train!'
- 'Blue!'
- 'Green!'
- 'Red truck!'
- 'Yellow brick!'
- 'Number two!'

It's not that you can't ever say these types of questions and comments, but focusing on them will restrict your conversations to asking questions that may never be answered or listing names of things, colors and numbers. And if your child can answer the questions, it's still not a natural conversation. They may be learned responses (Example: *'What does a dog say? Woof!'*). There may be missed opportunities to build a connection and introduce natural conversational language.

During play, these 'teachy' phrases we tend to model are the kinds of phrases that *we* want them to learn to say: they are still about what's in *our* head. These teachy phrases differ greatly from the 'kidspeak' phrases we saw earlier.

'Teacher mode' usually leads us to talk about colours, numbers and naming. This is great for academic learning but is often a dead end for conversation. If letters, colours, or numbers are of particular interest to your child then by all means, go ahead and talk about them because that is what they are interested in! But we also want to find a way to sneak in some natural conversation too (*'I like that red one! It's my favourite! This one's next! Oops, it fell down!' 'Number 7's coming up!'*). This is because our goal is to model communication, not teach numbers, colours or letters.

We may need to time our comments or reduce them if a child prioritises the sequence of reciting or doing an activity from beginning to end. Some children have a strong preference for naming things their way each time. They may walk away, turn their back, or really dislike you trying to get involved. In this case, regard that activity as their 'down time': what your child does to enjoy themselves and self-regulate. Other fun person-to-person games involving their favorite sensory thrills, like tickles, lifting them, clapping, 'dropping' them, or spinning them around may be better options to create fun connection with you, longer engagement with you, and opportunities for you to model more communication.

No definitive list of natural phrases or Gestalts can work for all children because every child has unique likes, dislikes, and experiences. And we need to match what we say to the moment, and that could be anything! Our mission is to try to fit as closely as possible whatever phrase or sound effect we can to their lightbulb moments – when they 'switch on', and something intriguing grabs their interest, when they are experiencing joy and are alert and connected to what's happening.

You'll also notice that we advise using 'I' or 'Me' in your Gestalts - as if you are using your child's voice. You literally need to be their voice, saying it as if they could say it themselves. This is because GLPs tend to process and learn exactly what they hear as a Gestalt, word for word. So we need to give them something from the outset that they can copy and have it work and make sense if they were to actually say it.

For example: if you ask '*Do you want some more?*' frequently during the day, and if your child latches onto this phrase and learns this as a Gestalt, then your child might eventually say '*Do you want some more?*' when they actually mean '*I really want some more*'. So '*Do you want some more?*' doesn't quite get across what they mean..

The words '*Let's*' or '*We*' are great ways to get around this, when you are modeling natural language for your child. This is because they cancel out the you/me confusion:

In our example, when we notice our child wanting more, we could say instead, '*Let's have some more!*' or '*We need some more!*' and then offer some more straight away without having any expectation for our child to do or say anything. Our child will then associate that phrase with the context of having some *more*. They may even say, '*Let's have some more*' or '*We need some more!*' or '*Some more*' to ask for more if and when they are ready. This kind of language is often what kids say naturally, for example: '*Let's play!*'.

Useful Phrase Examples

How do we know what to say to a GLP? How can we avoid falling into the 'question' or 'teachy' traps? To get you going, gather a list of useful words and phrases you can bring into your conversations regularly based on what your child usually likes or does. The aim is to comment naturally and match your message to whatever intrigues them.

If you pick a verb or action word like, '*Do / Did / Will / Can?*' Your sentence will automatically be a question - which we want to avoid for now! '*Do you want it? Did it work? Will we go? Can you jump?*'.

If you start with a *'Wh'* word, you'll also end up asking a question! *'Where is it? What is it? Who's that?'.*

We also want to avoid 'teachy' language like focusing on teaching colors and numbers, or even sounding like we are trying to teach something 'its a.... RED CAR!' This may or may not be what your child wants to talk about. We need to get out of our own head and focus on what *they* are interested in, not what we want to teach them.

Once you pick a way to start your phrase that isn't a question or 'teachy' language, your brain will figure out something naturally fitting to say about the play or the situation.

Some ideas for phrases can be:

- It's + (so big / really wet outside / bedtime / so much fun)
- There's + (a funny one / a yummy snack / my one)
- We + (need another one / can do it)
- Let's + (go outside / get another one / have a snack)
- That's + (my one / silly / yummy)
- I'm + (so hungry / so tired / gonna go now!)

For GLPs who are already starting to 'mix and match' phrase parts, it's also not just about changing up the end of the phrase. You could model the kinds of phrases where the beginning is a part that can swap out too:

- (I love / I'm all for / I'm going to do) + this!
- (This is / That's / Get) + my favorite one!

The words in brackets are ideas on how you could finish or start your phrases, depending on what is happening at the time. This is not a finite list: remember that your phrase will depend on what is happening. The ways to start or end the phrases are only examples; you want to come up with comments appropriate to what is happening at the time and hope that some of them stick or resonate with your child - with no expectation for them to either.

It is likely that you will accidentally start your language models with a *'Do?', 'Have?'* or *'Is?'* or use *'Wh'* questions and fall into the question trap! Become aware when this happens. There is a time when we focus on questions later on when they have more language. But early on, your child needs to hear lots of comments first. The chances are that even if you ask your GLP a question, it won't be answered (unless it is a learned response).

Be wary of 'tag' questions too: these are questions that we tag onto the end of our comments, for example: 'It's so big, *isn't it?*", 'I liked it, *didn't you?*'. These serve no purpose as they will often be ignored and don't really move the conversation forward. You could use the airtime instead to provide more useful language models. In addition, your child will likely focus on and process the last thing you say, so when you say, *'It's so big!'* they will hear the phrase. If you follow it up with *'Isn't it?'*, then that's what they will focus on and process first, and the original natural Gestalt (*'It's so big!'*) may get lost.

If you find yourself asking a question or a tag question, answer it yourself so it doesn't hang with nowhere to land: *'Where is it? Oh I found it!' 'Who's coming? I think it's Jim!'*. That way, your child has another opportunity to hear a relevant language model.

As your child tunes into the language models you are using, some of them will resonate or stick, and you may find your child using your intonation later on or even attempting to say some of them. When this happens, you can keep going with the fun and validate their messages (*'I like it too! / I see it! / That's what I thought!'*). If your child starts to really increase their use of Gestalts, you can then combine their Gestalts in your chat: 'I'm so hungry, let's get a snack!'.

Later again, you can start to break them up, especially if you notice your child beginning to do this naturally. For example, your child might create a new phrase by themselves like, '*I'm so + tired!*' then at another time: '*I'm so + happy!*'. This gives you license to use more of this type of phrase to show how it can be used in other new ways.

Other examples include: '*Let's get + some juice*' and, '*We need + some juice*'. It can be very powerful when you take one of their favorite phrases that they say, like '*It's a bit itchy!*' and use it to model how you can mix it up: '*It's a bit scratchy!*' when your child comes across something scratchy, of course. When you do this, you are modeling how Gestalts can be broken down into smaller chunks and recombined to make a new phrase.

Try to use silly or fun words when you can, whenever they fit the situation. These might include catchy phrases and sayings like:

- 'Uh oh!'
- 'Snug as a bug!'
- 'Bzzzz Bzzzz!'
- It's so cold... Brrrrrrr!'
- 'We're all done!'
- 'Let's go!'

You can also match phrases from their favorite show into suitable daily routines. For example, suppose a character from a favorite entertainment media clip regularly says, 'Come on, kids!' and you notice your child enjoys this by getting excited. In that case, you can mimic how the character says that phrase and use it when you are leaving the house to go out.

Key GLP Tip: Remember the practice you did to 'lift your voice'? This can be particularly helpful for some Gestalt Language Processors. When you lift your voice and are generally animated by putting emotion into your comments, it helps a Gestalt Language Processor connect with the music in the phrases you say and the interesting sounds you make. (Remember also that some children have sensitivities, so this may not work for them.)

Look interested, lean forward, and look as if you are waiting and watching for your child to do or say something next, but it doesn't matter if they don't. You are just showing them that you are present. You are also leaving space to see if something interesting happens that your child connects with; For example, when they start a new, unexpected way to play or if a distraction pulls their attention elsewhere. That is your cue to add your fun sound, word, or phrase to fit their experience.

Songs and music can also greatly interest young children who are GLPs and are to be encouraged, even if they don't usually join in. I remember one time when a parent lay down beside her child and started up a fun 'Go sleep (*'snore snore'*) Wake up!' short repeatable game. A few minutes later, the child moved on to another activity but was humming. We didn't notice it at the time, but when we looked back at a video recording of the event, we realized that he was humming a phrase from the *'Are you sleeping?'* song to do with waking up in the morning! That child made clever links and communicated in the way that was natural for him – through a musical Gestalt. This also demonstrates the power of video to help alert us to how they communicate.

Please see the resources at the end of this book for more information on the Natural Language Acquisition approach and seek the support of a GLP-aware Speech Therapist.

'RESPOND WITH ENTHUSIASM' VIDEO CHALLENGE

No matter whether your child is an Analytic or Gestalt Language Processor, Try to include fun sound effects and conversational phrases (unless they are not in the mood or dislike it from a sensory point of view). If you notice your child enjoying when you are animated with sound effects and conversational phrases and if they are in the mood, you really can't go wrong!

Record yourself now playing with your child for 2-3 minutes. Remember to start with all the previous strategies first:

- 'Get out of your own head', Get close and Watch your child quietly
- Figure out what they are interested then
- Get involved and have fun!
- Then Listen and pay special attention to your child's little sounds so that you can:
- Acknowledge (smile, nod, respond in some way: *'Really? Wow! That's cool!'*
- Model language based on what you think your child is interested in and 'Respond with Enthusiasm' (or 'Gentleness' if your child prefers this)
- Give it (if possible, for example, another puzzle piece or another few berries)

Don't continue until you have completed this video challenge.

When you look back at your video, see if there were specific times that you listened, acknowledged, and modeled language with enthusiasm (or gentleness).

1. Did you miss any little sounds that your child made?
2. Could you have paid more attention?
3. Could you have acknowledged your child's message differently?
4. Did you ask too many questions? What sound effect or comment could you have said instead?
5. Did you use any 'teachy' language? What sound effect or comment could you have said instead?
6. Did you respond with more enthusiasm or lift your voice, and how did your child respond?
7. Or did lower, gentler tones help to keep your child calmer instead?
8. Did you have a chance to point to something your child was already interested in to show that you could see it, too?
9. Could you have responded with other interesting sound effects or phrases?

Find an example in your video and write out how you could have:

Listened to my child's message

____

____

Acknowledged my child's message

____

____

Been more Enthusiastic (or adjusted my tone and animation)

____

____

Modeled a sound effect or fun phrase to fit what happened

____

____

Shown (pointed to or lifted up what I was talking about)

____

____

(Given it, if possible)

____

____

This is a tricky strategy to nail as there is so much involved. You are now trying to combine many strategies all at the same time. My advice is not to move on to the next strategy until you have spent at least a couple of weeks on all of the different aspects of the 'Respond with Enthusiasm (or Gentleness)' strategy, and it starts to become automatic.

Don't try to do too much at once: if you need to focus on one particular part of the strategy for a while, then focus on that.

You can practice by setting a two-minute timer on your phone. For those two minutes, focus on doing that one thing. Practice this regularly, several times a day, until it feels more natural. You may find you have an 'Aha!' moment where everything clicks into place, and it suddenly becomes effortless!

When combined, these important strategies help your child understand and link your words to their thoughts. This lets them feel more connected to you and experience how communication can be fun!

PASS IT ON!

Right at the start of this book, we talked about how a parent has such an important role in guiding their children, and part of that role is to share ideas so their kids can learn how communication works. I have seen countless times how small acts can have a huge impact, and this is why I wanted to write this book.

We often learn from our own and other people's mistakes. But mistakes aren't the only way we learn. We learn by trying things out, watching how others do things, practicing, and sharing what we know with each other. As a parent reading this book, you not only have a big chance to help your child but also to help other parents.

Think of Stephen Hawking, a brilliant physicist who, despite facing the challenges of a motor neuron disease, revolutionized our understanding of the cosmos. Hawking overcame significant communication barriers to make complex theories accessible to all. His perseverance and ability to convey abstract ideas in simple terms have inspired countless people.

While our journey is not quite on the same scale as Hawking's, the essence of your role is similar. The strategies you use, the experiences you gather, and the insights you share are crucial. You now have an opportunity to make a real difference in guiding other parents to help their own children.

By leaving a review of this book on Amazon, you'll show other parents where they can find the guidance they're looking for.

Simply by telling other readers how this book helped you and what they can expect to find inside, you'll set them on their own learning path to guide their own kids' communication to the next level.

Thank you so much for your support. You are still honing your own skills as early communication expert, but whatever direction you're heading in, this is a great start! Sharing our knowledge and experiences helps to make a real difference to people's lives.

Scan the QR link below:

5

STRATEGY 5: PAAAUUUSE...

Pausing is a whole strategy in itself: we have talked so much about what to say that it is easy to forget to pause! At this point, you may be trying to model language at the right level, while at the same time juggling to keep it fun, watching everything going on and coming up with a plan in the moment of what to say and do next, all at the same time! It would really help if you had time to gather your thoughts, to step back, and to watch your child. So, this is a timely reminder to pause and not say too much!

LET'S REVIEW

What are you pausing for? Firstly, holding back allows you to notice and capture the moment your child makes a little sound or movement so that you can respond with enthusiasm (or gentleness) and keep the interaction moving back and forth.

Secondly, your child needs time to process what is happening! You may have just said something fun and pointed. Your child needs time to take it all in, figure it out, make links, and internalize the experience.

As adults, we easily process what is going on around us. It is second nature to us; we do it automatically. But for our children, everything is new! There are also distractions like competing sounds, smells, things to look at, and the internal feelings of their own body. The toy may look like it's just falling to the floor to us, but your child might be focusing on how fast it drops, how the light catches it as it falls, or the sound it makes when it hits the ground. Practically everything they do involves learning something new for them.

Please don't fill the silence; your child needs it. That silence is just as important as any words you could say, if not more important.

THE 'PAUSE' MANTRA

It can be helpful at this stage to think of this as a repeatable process:

- Wait for my child to do or say something
- Respond with Enthusiasm
- Pause for 5 - 10 for seconds
- Wait for my child to do or say something
- Respond with Enthusiasm
- Pause for 5 - 10 for seconds

... And repeat!

Keep repeating this process over and over. If you say something, then something else immediately, and something yet again right after, will your child have time to process all those comments? No! The first one was enough... then pause. Then you can add your second comment. Pause again.... Then add your third one. At least your child will have an opportunity to process what you say and might even join in and say or do something if they wish.

Another reason for the pause after you say something is that your child has a chance to say or do something again, then you can say something else, then they can again, and so on. This sets up a pattern that mimics the flow of conversation back and forth, which is an important concept for your child to experience whether or not your child already has words. It builds the foundation for longer, fun connections.

Leaving space in the conversation through pausing has another significant benefit: When you do actually say something, no matter what you say, it will really stand out! Your child may be more alert to your comment than if you constantly say sounds or phrases with nowhere for them to land. Saying comments and questions back to back with no pausing may seem like a wall of sound to your child, and they may tune it out.

When you do the video challenge and pause during the play, you will think your pause is reeeaaaally long. But when you look back at your video, count the exact number of seconds you waited. Guaranteed, you'll think you have waited about 10 or 15 seconds, but it might actually be about 2 or 3 seconds, maybe 4 or 5 at a stretch! This is where you need to practice giving yourself time to pause consciously. You can count to 5 or 10 in your mind at a slow pace to help you hold back. Less is more!

'PAUSE' VIDEO CHALLENGE:

Record yourself playing with your child. Make sure you put all the previous strategies into action first, then start to pause.

Remember to follow the Pause Mantra!

→Wait →Respond →Pause for 5-10 seconds

→Wait →Respond →Pause for 5-10 seconds

And so on!

Don't worry too much about what you respond with for this challenge. Anything that sounds fun is good! You are trying to get a rhythm or flow going so that it becomes natural for you to pause more. Another reason is that your child may choose to fill that pause with something from their communication repertoire, which means they are initiating interaction or communication more! If they do, then respond to what they said or did in a fun way.

It's time to try the challenge and then come back, watch your video, and reflect on the questions below.

When you look back at your video, ask yourself these questions:

1. Did you remember to pause?
2. For how long did you actually wait - how many seconds exactly?
3. Did you wait long enough?
4. How did your child respond?
5. Did they take a turn by either doing or saying something?

6. Did you jump in too soon so your child didn't have a chance to do or say something?
7. How hard was it to pause?
8. How can you remind yourself to hold back more to give your child a chance to do or say something? (Remember, they don't have to.)

You can note your answers and reflections here:

____

____

____

____

Many parents find that they are doing too much talking when they look back at their video. If this sounds like you, don't beat yourself up over it. It is a natural thing that many of us do! But now that you know this is your default position, you can do something about it and focus on practicing pausing more. Record yourself daily and practice pausing for 5-10 seconds until it becomes natural and easy as pie.

In this chapter you learned…

- pausing is just as important as modeling sounds and words
- we typically underestimate the length of time that we pause
- pausing helps a child to process what is happening and what is being said
- pausing means your child can really tune into the sounds and words you do say

- the pause mantra: wait for my child to do or say something, respond with enthusiasm, pause for 5 - 10 for seconds then repeat this process
- pause between comments instead of saying comments back to back
- pausing allows the space for your child to potentially take a turn naturally by themselves if they wish

6

STRATEGY 6: 10-20 SECOND 'SHORT REPEATABLE GAMES'

Short Repeatable Games are the kind of quick, fun games you can repeat several times in the space of one minute, like tickles, chasing, or 'lift me up!'. The main goal of these games is to create as much joy as possible for your child. If your child is up for sharing that joy with you, then you can create structure with predictable steps so that it becomes even more fun and exciting for both of you. During these games, you are not demanding anything from your child other than for them to show you if it is fun for them. You allow them the space to express themselves if they wish to, but nothing is dependent on them doing or saying something in a particular way for them to have fun in the game!

Many of these games can involve movement, like running, lifting or jumping, but they can arise from following whatever your child is interested in. It is often best if these games evolve organically from applying all the previous strategies together when you notice your child is interested in or enjoying something and then go with it. If you notice your child likes a particular action or event, try to repeat it and see if your child enjoys the repetition of it.

For example, suppose you notice your child is interested in how the cupboard door in the kitchen sounds as they open and close it. In that case, you can join in opening and closing another door. You can turn it into a 'knock knock' game - if this is something that creates even more joy for your child. Or if your child enjoys hiding in a small cupboard under the stairs, you could turn it into a 'peek-aboo' game, 'Knock knock! Where's Johnny? Found you!!'. Again, only do this if you find your child enjoys it and watch for signs that they are open to the fun you are adding. The games we just mentioned could be repeated over and over many times in one minute.

It is very important to name your game! And add a hand gesture where possible. We suggest this so your child can anticipate what game is about to be played and start connecting the words and actions with it. So for the example of the child who likes hiding under the stairs: When you see your child going to hide in their favorite place, you could say, 'Let's play Peekaboo!' or 'Let's play Boo!' and make a peeping action with your hands each time, just before you play a 'peekaboo' game with them - as long as they enjoy playing this game with you. Later on, your child might start to ask for the game with an attempt at 'boo' or 'peekaboo' or copy the peeping action you made to let you know they want to play that game. Or they might pull you by the hand to where they like to play the game.

It is also important for minimally speaking children that you don't vary what you say during each step of your game so that your child learns what your words mean. Stick to saying a limited number of predictable phrases for each game, for example, four or five phrases. Try to have something to say for each step during your game. Your short repeatable game must ideally be long enough to have a 'fun bit' that your child enjoys, but short enough that you can repeat it quickly and many times over. We will go through some examples of this in the next section.

'Solo Goes'

At first, you will need to take a few turns alone with no expectation that your child will do or say anything: They get to enjoy all the fun! This is so that they get to know how the game works. So remember to include 'Solo Goes' any time you start a game for about the first 2 to 3 turns. You can also throw in some 'Solo Goes' if your child starts to lose interest. When you offer a few solo goes back to back, it may help to extend the fun and leave it on a high note for your child.

SHORT REPEATABLE GAMES WITH MOVEMENT

A great way to engage your child is with movement games - if they enjoy them. These are the games that get their body moving because we know that movement leads to communication opportunities. Your child is alert, and their senses are being stimulated by being in different positions, feeling where their body is in space, how fast they are moving, and how parts of their body are moving relative to the rest of their body. Your child may love games involving speed when running around, height when lifted, or being turned upside down!

The list of these types of games is endless, but remember that you must adapt the activities or games your own child likes using the *principles* of the following examples. Do not just play the games in the examples below with your child because your child may not enjoy these particular games. Whatever you focus on must be fun for *them*, and you should know this from doing Strategy 1.

Here are a few examples with suggested steps and ideas for language you could add for each step to stay consistent:

Gonna Getcha' Game:

1. Gonna getcha'! (I chase my child with arms outstretched) *(Could pause here before catching your child)*
2. 'Gotcha!' (I catch my child with my arms)
3. Big squeeeeeeze'! (we have a big hug with the 'squeeeeeze!' or tickle + sound effect) *(Could pause here before letting your child go again)*
4. 'Gonna Getcha!' (I let go with my arms and chase again, arms outstretched)
5. Repeat several times in one to two minutes

'Gonna Getcha' is a common short repeatable game. It is possible to repeat this game many times within the space of one or two minutes. During this game, you are looking to see if your child anticipates you catching and squeezing them. But first, you need to show your child how the game works: The routine has to be established. This is also where you get to take the lead and show each step while keeping the pace going. Try to do several rounds of the game - these are your 'Solo Goes' where your child doesn't need to do anything, and you make all the fun happen for them, following the same steps and using the same language each time. So if you already play some established games with your child, you can adapt your game to have consistent language for each step, then go ahead and give some 'Solo Goes' of the new format of the game so they get used to it.

The best games emerge organically out of random things you notice in the moment. So start with Strategy 1, 'get out of my own head', get close and watch'. You may notice something new that your child really enjoys. Now you can decide on the structure of your game. What is the most fun part for your child? In our example, it could be the 'catching' and the squeeze! Alternatively, it could be when you let them go, and they get to run around again! It depends on your child's preference, which you can figure out by watching their reactions. When you have identified the most fun part for your child, you will know when to pause - before that fun part! In that pause, you are offering space to your child to say or do something, but the next step is not dependent on it - the fun thing will happen anyway!

You will need to write down what you will say for each step. This may not happen the first time you play the game, as you'll be too busy playing it! But you can reflect on it afterward and define each step and what you could say to be consistent. Then, write down your steps and exactly what you will say. You will want to introduce the game the same way ('Gonna Getcha!') and make the same actions, sounds, words, and comments each time. Writing everything down will help you stay consistent so that the game becomes predictable for your child. We need predictability so your child can learn to anticipate the steps, and then they will know what words are coming too and learn what they mean. Eventually, they might take a turn and voluntarily do or say something within the game.

Once you have written out all the steps, gestures you'll make, and words you'll say, you are ready to play the game with your child. You may need to wait until they show an interest in the game again.

If you find that your child is having fun with you in the game, remember that you can take charge of the steps by making the steps happen, and your child doesn't need to do or say anything. These are your 'Solo Goes' where you take charge, and they have all the fun!

Then, once you have run through a few 'Solo Goes' and demonstrated a few turns, you can start to slow down and pause during the activity - the best time to stop is just before the most fun part of the game. You should have identified this from observing your child before. We have two possible pause points in our example, but only stop once before what you think is the most fun part for your child.

Once you introduce a pause in the game before the most fun part, you are looking to see if your child anticipates any of the steps in the game. Do they come looking for you, expecting the squeeze, and then know when to run off? Do they look for the game to continue? If so, how? Do they join in by doing something physical to ask for more, make sounds, or say any of the sound effects, words, or phrases?

Calling the routine the 'Gonna Getcha' game makes sense. When you say 'Gonna Getcha', it's catchy, and your child will instantly recognize what that means – chasing. You can also pretend to run by moving your arms as you say, 'Gonna Getcha!', so your child can do the action to ask for the game, or they might just run off giggling. Or they might use the intonation that you normally use in your voice but without words, so listen out carefully for your child's sounds and how they babble or chatter. It likely has some associated meaning!

Here are some more examples of common short repeatable games:

'Up! Up! Up!' Game:

1. I see my child climbing me, maybe looking up at me or putting their arms out to be lifted
2. I say, 'Up up up!' with my arms outstretched
3. I lift my child up and say, '*Wheeeeee!*' (or something similar). I can do something fun that my child likes – a tickle, for example. (This is the fun bit that may encourage them to want more of this game!)

4. I put my child down again and say, '*All the way doooooowwwwwn!*'
5. I pause and watch for signs that my child wants *'up'* again. They might climb, look up, reach up to ask for the game again
6. I could also pause momentarily before I give the tickle to see if my child asks for it in some way
7. Repeat a few times in one to two minutes

This game is also practical, short and repeatable. The fun bits during this game are going up and getting a tickle. So when you put your child down again, they might immediately look to go up again by saying something or putting out their arms. If your child enjoys the tickle, they may do or say something to look for the tickle, too! Plus, an added bonus: this is your workout for the week!

If your child doesn't respond, it could be because they don't want to play anymore, which is okay. You could go back to giving 'Solo Goes', where you take over and do all the steps again for a few rounds. Or you could wait a little longer and see if your child requests 'up' again by saying something, holding out their arms, or some other way.

A variation on this game is to spin around instead of the tickles, once you have lifted your child. Again be guided by what your child likes.

Tickles:

1. I get close to my child, possibly above them, while they lie on the bed or in front of them on the couch

2. I say, *'Gonna Tickle!'* and raise my arms. I might say *'Aaaaaahhhh!'* to build the excitement just before I jump in with some tickles!
3. I go to tickle and say, *'Tickle tickle tickle!'* as I'm tickling
4. I say *'Stop!'* and suddenly pull my hands back but keep them raised with a fun expression on my face
5. Once I have run through a few 'Solo Goes', this is the point I can wait a few seconds
6. If my child doesn't do anything, I start again and repeat, and watch for any message my child sends to ask for more tickles so I can respond

Peekaboo!

1. I can use a blanket over my head or my child's head or use my hands to hide my face
2. I say, 'Where's....? (my child's name / or my name)
3. I don't wait too long for the first few times. When my child knows the game, I can wait a little longer to see if my child will do the next step. I'll accept any response on their first attempt
4. My child or I will take off the blanket, and I say, 'Peekaaaa...boo!'. Later when my child knows the game and is showing signs that they are ready to take a turn, I can stop after 'Peekaaa....' And see if they join in for 'Boo!' But if they don't, I make the fun thing happen anyway
5. Repeat

If you have a phrase like 'Peekaboo', it is important that someone finishes the 'Peeka...' with a 'Boo!' each time. You don't want to repeat 'Peeka...' several times in a row without a 'Boo'. Or you don't want to leave the 'Peeka....' hanging, or else your child won't realize that the 'Boo' is part of the same sound effect and might think of 'Peeka...' and 'Boo!' as two separate words or units. The same applies to 'Ready steady Go' or '1 2 3 Go' or any other phrase with the quality of a Gestalt. This is especially important early on.

'Drop' or 'Crash'

1. Let's play Crash!'
2. I lift my child and prepare them for the drop onto the big pillow by counting 1, 2, 3.... (This is where I could pause after a few solo goes)
3. I say *'Crassshhhh!'* and I carefully drop my child onto the pillow so he feels the pressure of landing
4. Repeat!

Consider the ideas we have mentioned and see if they can be adapted to your child. Make a list of some of your ideas and add structure to create your short repeatable games so you can practice some of them right away! See if your child enjoys them.

Your child might need to learn the Short Repeatable Game first, so don't expect them to join immediately. You should lead the game and keep the pace going with a few 'Solo Goes' so they can learn each step. If your child loses interest, you can revert back to 'Solo Goes' to keep the flow going, too.

Don't forget to give a few 'Solo Goes' at first: When a short repeatable game emerges from the fun play, and you manage to complete one round of your repeatable game, try to keep the momentum moving when that first round is over so that you can squeeze a few rounds of it into that first minute! If you wait too long after the first round is finished, your child may lose interest. So, introduce the repetition and keep it going for a few rounds without any expectations.

Remember to follow the same format each time you do a round of your short repeatable game: If you vary the steps or words each time, will your child get a handle on the sequence of steps properly? Probably not, and you will also want to keep using consistent language for the steps of your game so that predictability helps your child learn what the words mean. Your child might even attempt to do or say something when they are ready.

After your child knows exactly what the game involves, you can add drama like parents naturally do. This means you can add excitement: Ideally, before the bit your child enjoys the most, build up a little bit of fun anticipation so your child has the most fun experience ever!

So for the 'Gonna Getcha' game, that might be after you catch and squeeze them. Linger a little by continuing to hold them after the squeeze part to see if they want to run off again and how they communicate that to you. But let them go anyway either way!

For the 'Up Up Up' game, pause after you have left them down again. If they are already nailing the reaching up or asking for more in some other way, you could also add a pause before the tickle. You could wait to see if they move their body, make a sound, or communicate they want the tickle in another way. If they do, then you can make a big fuss with tickles! If they don't request it, tickle them anyway and move on quickly, so you have another opportunity for your child to connect with you and communicate something on your next round.

They might even giggle or make a sound with their voice. If they do, then this is your cue to go 'all in' and make that fun part happen with a LOT of enthusiasm in the most fun way possible! Your child will have a great time, and you will too! Big tickles! Big Squeezes! Fun throws in the air! Whatever the fun part of your short repeatable game is, make it super fun and last a bit longer. If your child doesn't make a sound or move their body or ask for it again in some way, then still give them the fun bit. Remember, we never withhold anything. Move forward quickly though, so that you can start the game again and build up to the next fun pause when they can have another opportunity to communicate something to you.

So your job while you play with your child is to continue watching and listening to them closely so that you notice what they like, and then you can make a game out of it for extra fun. Your job is also to notice those little attempts to communicate with you in whatever way so that you can catch that moment and respond straight away - responding to their *first* attempt to communicate. Remember also to respond with even more enthusiasm if you hear sounds or word attempts so that you can validate their power to use their own voice.

QUICK CHALLENGE

Think of a list of movement games your child likes to do with you. How could you turn them into Short Repeatable Games with structure? Write out each step. What language could you add for each step? What could you call your game? Is there a gesture you could add to show what the game is when you say the name of your game?

Keep your 'recipe' for your short repeatable game easily accessible when you play it. Write with a thick pen on a sticky that you can put on the wall so that you can see it from across the room. That way, you'll be able to keep your game consistent and will have more head space and energy to spend watching and listening out for your child's communication attempts so you can respond quickly.

SHORT REPEATABLE GAMES WITH TOYS OR OBJECTS

Here are some more examples of short repeatable games that might emerge from playing with toys:

Poke Game

If your child likes poking sand with a tool, for example, then you could say, '*Poke poke poke!*' as you poke the sand and then pause to see if your child will copy you. If they don't, then start saying '*Poke poke poke*' again as you poke the sand, then pause again. The sound could add more fun to the activity they already enjoy.

Squish Game

If your child likes squishy textures, do the same as the 'Poke' game, only this time you can say 'squish squish squish!' or 'squishy!'. You could squish your child if they like that sensation. If not, then just join in 'squishing' the textures and making fun sounds, followed by pausing.

Push Game

If your child likes to press buttons on toys, you could do a big pointing action or another big gesture as you approach to press some buttons and say a fun sound like 'Bop!' or 'Bing!' to match the sound of the button, and then pause. Watch for your child's reactions. You can start again and see if they notice or begin to copy you. If they don't, then repeat the game again, as long as they are happy for you to.

In and Out (with Objects)

If your child likes to put things in and out of containers, have the two containers they normally use. If your child tolerates it, you can put the wrong thing into the wrong box ('*Uh oh!*') and then wait... and see how your child responds. They may not notice at all! Or they may notice and react in some way. If disrupting their game upsets your child, do not persist with it. If they grumble a bit, help them to see that your intention is to have fun by being animated, smiling and showing that it's fun: '*Uh oh! Silly Mommy!*'. Quickly follow it up by handing them the thing they want and letting them carry on as they wish. Then, in a few more turns, do the silly thing again! And wait to see how your child responds.

Another way to play 'In and Out' could be to comment as you put the object in the box and make a big gesture, raising your arm up high and slowly lowering it into the box as you say, '*Going going going IN!*' or something equally catchy! Next time, you can pause just after the 'Going going going....' And then pause so you can highlight when you say the 'in' part. You could do the same for the 'out' part and say: '*Take it, take it, take it... OUT!*' The catchy phrase you use doesn't have to be this. Just say something you might naturally say in a catchy way. Then, you can pause before the last part to allow your child to process your words and maybe do something or say something like joining in as you say, 'In' and 'Out' in our example.

An alternative version is to quickly put something 'in and out' in a play-acting way. '*Gonna put it... IN, gonna take it... OUT / in OUT in OUT!*' as you do the actions, then wait and repeat. See if your child likes this game, and if they notice you, copy or communicate something. This can work well for children who really enjoy the speed element.

In and Out (Me!)

If your child likes getting in and out of things physically, like a tent, then you can add structure by sitting with your child as they get in, then gently close the entrance and ask, '*Where's (+your child's name)?' "Here I am!'*, and open the entrance with excitement. Remember, you can use I/ me as if you are their voice if your child is a Gestalt Language Processor (See Strategy 4). This could also turn into a 'Peekaboo' game if your child enjoys it.

1 2 3 Splash!

The Splash game is one for a hot, sunny day! If you have a hose in your yard and know that your child enjoys being doused by water, you can spray your child a few times! Add language like '*Ready.. here we go! ...Splash!*'. Then start to wait. See if your child wants some more by how they communicate with you. What if they don't communicate intentionally using their body or voice? In that case, you can still douse them again, but react immediately if you see them indicating they want more, especially if you hear them make any sound or word attempt! The language you can add could be: '*Let's splash!*' '*Splash!*' '*More Splashes!*' '*All wet!*' '*Let's splash again!*' and so on.

Go Sleep, Wake Up!

If your child likes to lie on the floor, you can say, '*I'm SO tired! I'm gonna go sleep!*' and lie down with them. Pretend to sleep. Make snoring sounds and then exclaim, '*Wakey wakey!*' or '*Wake Up!*', then repeat the game a few more times as 'Solo Goes': '*I'm SO tired*' *(snore sounds)* '*Wake up!*'. After a few of your 'Solo Goes', you can add a pause when you are pretending to sleep and see if your child will prompt you to 'wake up!' by pushing you, tickling you, making sounds, or saying the words. You can also play this game pretending to make Teddy go sleep and wake up. If your child uses random little sounds or word attempts, you can wake up in an extra fun way to validate the power of using their voice.

Oh No! Games

Games that involve an 'Oh No!' moment are great for adding drama and turning into Short Repeatable Games. Why do many children seem to enjoy 'oh no' games so much? Often, they involve a problem that needs to be fixed, like in the stories children enjoy hearing or seeing in books. Usually, there is a character who has a problem that ends up getting fixed at the end of the storybook. So when you act out Short Repeatable 'Oh No!' games, you are following that pattern. You are looking during the play for something that can go 'wrong' - *'Oh no! It's gonna fall!', 'Oh no! Dolly's thirsty!', 'Oh no! Teddy's hungry!', 'Oh no! Monkey's tired!'.*

IMPORTANT: If your child does not enjoy the playfulness of this type of game, do not persist. We only want to play games that are fun for your child. We do not want to upset them. If it is not fun, then they are not feeling joy, connecting with you, or learning. It would help if you watched your body language closely during 'Oh No!' games. You can help your child understand that the 'Oh No!' is not serious and is only pretend by smiling and raising your eyebrows as you say the 'Oh No!' and keeping your tone upbeat. This sends a clear message that there is nothing to worry about. Some children can become unsure, worried or upset if you say, 'Oh No!' with a slight frown. They can be so good at reading body language that they interpret your facial expression first. They may incorrectly interpret your frown to mean that something bad is happening! Keep smiling all the way through, and keep it playful.

Of course, you can come up with plenty of your own 'Oh No!' Short Repeatable Games: don't just follow the ones mentioned here. Please adapt them and make up your own as long as your child is having fun and feels safe. These examples aim to demonstrate how to construct a Short Repeatable Game with a pause for your child to communicate something when they are ready. Let's take a look at some of these ideas:

1. Crash!

A simple game that many children like is to play 'crash' with toy cars or trucks. If your child is interested in this type of game, you can get it started by going close to your child when they start playing with cars, then do a few crashes and say, '*Crash!' Oh nooo! He fell over!*' Then pause to see what your child might do or say. As your child becomes more and more engaged, pull back and leave space for them to crash their car into yours or make sounds if they wish. If they make a sound or word attempt, respond with enthusiasm! Don't worry if they don't react, and carry on playing as long as they are enjoying the fun.

2. Oh No! Monkey's Soooo Tired!

If your child has a stuffed toy they like, for example, a toy monkey, then you can act out this game: '*Monkey is sooo tired, oh no! He needs a rest!*' Put Monkey to bed with some snoring noises, then say, 'Wake up, Monkey!'. Monkey wakes up and does something fun (tickles or does lots of jumping around). Then Monkey can suddenly be 'so tired' again, and you can repeat it. After a few 'Solo Goes', you can wait to see if your child will wake Monkey up and how they do it. If they make a sound, respond with enthusiasm!

3. Oh No! Teddy's Hungry!

This game follows a similar pattern to the 'so tired' game. If your child starts playing with the teddy or something similar, you can say, '*Oh No! Teddy's hungry!*'. You can even 'be the voice' of the teddy, 'I'm soooo hungry! Where's my lunch?' and then act out feeding him '*Nom nom nom*'. He might even nibble on your child's fingers, tummy or toes. Then you can say, '*Ahhh! I'm full up now!*'. Then quickly go back to '*Oh No! I'm sooo hungry again!*'.

4. Oh No! The Train's Stuck!

If your child likes pushing a train around the track, then this might be a fun one for them. You can place something (a truck, a doll, etc.) across the track. '*Oh no! The trains stuck!*'. See if your child likes this game and if they respond to the fun. If they don't, then lift it within a few seconds. *'Phew! He's freeeeee!' Yay!'*. You can repeat this to see if your child learns the game and anticipates what will happen next. This may not be fun for GLPs who may like to play the same way every time; in this case, do not persist. But some children really enjoy the added element of intrigue, and it adds to their enjoyment of the game. This kind of play also brings them closer to early pretend play.

5. Oh No! I'm stuck!

This game is good for children who like slides. You can playfully put your arm across the slide as they sit at the top. This means they can't get down! You can say, *'Oh No! I'm stuck!'*. You can quickly lift the 'barrier' (your arm) and let your child down without delay for a few turns. You can say something like *'Go go go!'* or whatever you would normally say in a natural way. Then, when your child knows the game, you can leave the barrier down for a few extra seconds and add the drama *'Oh No! What will we do?!'*. See if your child does or says anything to get the barrier up again. But lift it anyway within a few seconds if they don't react and say *'Go go go!'* or something else fun. Remember to watch and listen for any little sounds or word attempts, raise your arm immediately, and respond with enthusiasm if you hear anything at all. You will be showing them that their voice is important by responding to their little unintentional sounds. But lift the barrier anyway within a few seconds, even if they don't make a sound or communicate in another way. Stay playful at all times without expecting or demanding a particular response.

Songs

Songs are natural and powerful, 'Short Repeatable Games'. You can use songs in several ways:

1. You can sing the song your child likes, such as '*The Wheels on the Bus*'; your child could join in with some of the actions. In this case, you can pause before the word associated with the action. Wait to see if your child will do the action; if they don't, you can do the action anyway. Sometimes, children like to put their hand on top of your hand as you do the actions. This is a great step! Taking their hand and making them do it is not recommended, as this takes away from their bodily autonomy, or their control over their own body. So it is better if they voluntarily choose to put their hand or hands on yours.

2. If your child takes an interest in your singing and anticipates parts of the song, you can start to pause before the last word of each line. So in the case of 'Humpty Dumpty' for example:

> Humpty Dumpty sat on a .....? Waaaallll!
> Humpty Dumpty had a great.....? Faaaallll!
> All the King's horses and all the King's.....? Meeennnn!
> Couldn't put Humpty together......? Agaaaaain!

It is important to emphasize the last word as you sing it, as this will send the message to your child that this is the part they can join in on if and when they are ready. Gestalt Language Processors may start to hum or sing entire lines. In that case, alternate lines with them instead of the last word. If possible, add an action or a type of movement your child enjoys into the song, as in our next point. Actions may be easier for your child to join in with, and movements may be fun for them.

3. You can turn any song into a movement game by adding one of their favorite movements. You could bounce your child up and down on your knee while you sing, '*Horsey, horsey, don't you stop!*'. Or you can sing '*Wheels on the Bus Go Round and Round*' while spinning your child around with you for the 'round and round' bit. Or

you can bounce your child on your knees and include a drop: for example, when Humpty has a great *'fall'* or in '*Rock-a-bye Baby*' you could drop your child between your knees on the last word *'all'* when you sing '*Down will come baby cradle and all*'.

4. You can make the song more personal by changing the words to include your child's name: '*Down will come Jamie, cradle and all!*'.

5. You can change words in any song to make it about a routine or game: '*This is the way we wash wash wash*' to the tune of '*Here We Go Round The Mulberry Bush*', or if your child likes jumping you could sing '*Jumping jumping 1 2 3!*' to the tune of '*Twinkle Twinkle Little Star*'. You could sing '*Brush brush brush your teeth*' to the tune of '*Row Row Row your Boat*'. If you decide to adapt the words, keep it simple and repeat the main idea through your new song, as in the examples above. Don't add in too many new words. Try to make the main action stand out in the song. So if you are singing about 'brushing' hair, then 'brush' or 'brushing' is the word you should repeat. For example, to the tune of '*Row your Boat*', you could sing: '*Brush brush brush your hair, brush brush your hair*' and so on.

Remember that you are going with whatever is fun for your child. If they are not interested in the songs, you can still include them as part of your daily routines, but we know not to expect them to join in. If they enjoy the songs, you may add some pauses to allow space for them to process and join in, in whatever way is natural for them.

Songs Resources

Here is a list of common nursery rhymes that you can adapt to your needs by replacing the words to suit what you are doing:

- Alphabet song (Great for GLPs who like letters!)
- BINGO ('Clap clap clap-clap-clap' for example)

- Brother John (Are You Sleeping?)
- Five Fat Sausages
- Five Little Monkeys (Great for joining in with the actions!)
- Head, Shoulders, Knees and Toes (Great for learning body parts, add tickles and fun hand movements to make it extra fun)
- Here We Go Round the Mulberry Bush (Great for adapting words to suit your needs: This is the way we ('brush our teeth', 'wash our hands', 'go to sleep'....)
- Hey Diddle Diddle
- Hickery Dickery Dock (Great for joining in on the last word when ready e.g. 'clock' 'dock')
- Hokey Pokey
- Horsey Horsey Don't You Stop
- Hot Cross Buns
- Humpty Dumpty (Great for bouncing on your knee and dropping between your knees for the 'fall'. You can pause before the 'fall' and see if they anticipate it by moving their body or saying something!)
- Hush Little Baby
- I'm a Little Teapot (Great for actions)
- I saw a Ship A-Sailing
- If You're Happy and You Know It (Great for doing the 'clapping hands' actions!)
- It's Raining It's Pouring
- Itsy Bitsy Spider / Eensy Weensy Spider
- Jack and Jill
- Little Bo Peep
- Little Jack Horner
- Little Miss Muffet
- Mary Had a Little Lamb (Adapt the words to any daily routine: 'Let's go up and brush our teeth, brush our teeth,

brush our teeth!' or 'Wash, wash, wash our hands, wash our hands, wash our hands!')

- Mary Mary, Quite Contrary
- Old MacDonald Had a Farm
- Old Mother Hubbard
- One Finger One Thumb (Great for those children who like fingers!)
- One Two Three For Five (Great for GLPs who like numbers!)
- Oranges and Lemons
- Pat-a-Cake (Great for adding Gestures / Actions / Clapping)
- Polly Put the Kettle On
- Pop Goes The Weasel (You could adapt the words when blowing bubbles to 'Pop goes the bubble')
- Rain Rain Go Away
- Ring a Rosie (Great to stop and wait before the 'down' to see if your child will 'fall')
- Rock-a-by Baby (Great if a child likes dolls, they can join in with the actions)
- Round and Round the Garden (Great for those who like tickles and to help them anticipate the fun part!)
- Row Row Row Your Boat (Adapt the words to daily routines: 'Brush Brush Brush Your Teeth' or 'Wash Wash Wash your hands)
- Ten Green Bottles
- Ten Little Fingers
- The Grand Old Duke Of York (Great for moving legs' up' and 'down' if they are lying on their back)
- The More We Get Together
- The Wheels On The Bus (Great for doing actions your child can join in with!)
- This Little Piggy (Great for those who like fingers or toes)

- This Old Man (Adapt the words, for example: 'Let's go out, let's go out, let's get dressed and let's go out!')
- Twinkle Twinkle Little Star (Adapt the words, for example: 'Jumping jumping 1 2 3')
- Wind the Bobbin Up (Great for doing actions that children can join in with)

QUICK CHALLENGE

Make a list of other kinds of activities that your child likes to do. This could be movement games, games with toys or a song. Can you come up with some ideas for turning a high point of each activity into a Short Repeatable Game with structure? Which part is most fun for your child so you can pause just beforehand? Could you add a fun element that you can repeat each time and pause before? Write out the steps and exactly when you can stop. What reaction are you expecting from your child?

'SHORT REPEATABLE GAME' VIDEO CHALLENGE 1

For this challenge, record yourself playing with your child for 2 or 3 minutes, but you might want to wait for your child to show signs of wanting to play one of the repeatable games they already like. Then grab your recording device and get recording so that you can capture it. Do what you normally do for your short repeatable game. Make sure that you capture several rounds of it over a couple of minutes. The work will take place afterwards when you reflect on it. You will think of how to add even more structure to your game so you can get the most out of it. Stop reading now and wait for your child to want to do one of their favourite short repeatable games and record it. Do not go on until you have completed this Video Challenge.

I hope you had lots of fun! Now look back over your video and ask yourself the following questions:

1. What was the name of your game? Or if it doesn't have a name, what could you call it? Could you add a gesture?
2. What were the steps in your game?
3. Was each step clear?
4. Did you say the same sound effects or phrases for each step, or did you vary what you said?
5. Could you be more consistent? What could you say each time?
6. What is the most fun part of your short repeatable game for your child?
7. Could you add a better fun element?
8. When could you add a pause before the fun part to see if your child takes a turn some way?
9. How might your child ask for it? (Check the Communication Repertoire)
10. How can you help yourself remember to notice and Respond with Enthusiasm to their vocal attempts when they make a random sound or request more with their voice?

You can write your thoughts here:

___

___

___

___

'SHORT REPEATABLE GAME' VIDEO CHALLENGE 2

We have a second video challenge for this strategy. Yay! So now the goal is to follow all the strategies as before, but this time you will not watch and wait in quite the same way… instead you will try to find a brand new fun routine! You will not choose something for your child. You are going to follow these steps first:

- Get out of my own head, Get close and Watch my child quietly
- Figure out what they are interested in (the fluff on the floor, the way the lightbulb looked when you turned it off, the way the book looks funny upside down), then
- Get involved and have fun!
- Find the fun thing your child likes that you can repeat and turn into a short repeatable game!

Once you have noticed what your child likes, you will think of how to do something fun with it and turn it into a short, repeatable game…. Be creative! And watch your child closely to see their reactions when you try to repeat the fun thing. Now, this may or may not work out. Your child might not like the game, it may not sustain their interest enough, or they may not 'get' what you're trying to do. That's okay! It's all trial and error.

Finding new games to play with your child, based on their preferences, is a great goal. This will help expand your child's horizons, help them hear new language and learn what the words and phrases mean. We want to create new opportunities in fun new situations so your child can continue learning and expanding their skills over time.

So once you have identified a fun thing that excites them or makes them smile, try to find a way to repeat it. We are looking for something intriguing to do to create joy, make them giggle again or keep their interest going. Keep trying to repeat it as long as your child is having fun. Try to add some sound effects and phrases, and keep it consistent if you do get to do a few rounds of it. You don't need to add in your pause yet. Just get the flow going with some 'Solo Goes'. Your child needs to learn what the new game is first and all the steps that are involved. You can come back and practice this a few times to get better and better at spotting opportunities. Stop reading now and complete the challenge before moving on.

How did your video challenge go?

1. Did your child enjoy the game or not?
2. How did they show they liked it?
3. How did it feel for you: was it easy or difficult to spot what they really liked and to think in the moment?

4. Is this particular game something your child would like to revisit over and over again and add to their play repertoire?
5. Write out the steps of this new game and what you can say for each step. This will help you to keep them consistent as long as your child enjoys the game!
6. Is there a fun bit in the game that you could pause before?
7. How might your child take a turn before the fun bit? (Check the Communication Repertoire)
8. What are you going to watch or listen out for?
9. How will you respond if your child makes a little sound or attempts to say something?

You can write down your thoughts here:

____

____

____

____

Now that you have tried it out, what do you think is the value of Short Repeatable Games for your child? Does your child connect well with you during these games? Does your child engage for longer with you during these games? Is this something you can develop more to give your child even more opportunities to connect and communicate with you?

In this chapter, you learned...

- what a short repeatable game is
- the best short repeatable games emerge naturally from what your child already enjoys or from something spontaneous that your child enjoys in the moment

- it is vital to run through the short repeatable game several times with some 'Solo Goes' first so your child can learn the steps of the game, where you make all the fun happen without any expectation
- short repeatable games can be based around movement games or play with toys, objects or songs and rhymes
- short repeatable games involve predictability which lays the ground for your child to join in when ready
- writing down the steps, the words and sound effects you can say can help your child to predict what will come next

7

STRATEGY 7: SOUND EFFECTS!

Adding sounds or words that sound really 'catchy' can be incredibly effective in getting your child's attention and can create a situation where they may repeat something fun-sounding after you! Especially if you include sound effects in a fun 'Short Repeatable Game'.

You can turn sounds, words or phrases into sound effects by exaggerating them, making them longer or shorter or by making them stand out using repetition. You can also make them sound interesting by lifting your voice up or gliding your voice down. Of course, if your child prefers low key quieter sounds then you'll focus on adapting your sounds to whatever they enjoy, this could mean more bassy quiet sounds.

You are already doing this every day! We are just thinking through some examples so that you can expand your repertoire and bring them into your everyday interactions with your child in a more planned way.

Here are some examples:

- Poke poke poke!
- Swissssshhhhhhh
- One two threeeeeeee!
- Splaaassshhhh!
- Craaasshhhh!
- Tick! Tock! Tick! Tock!
- Booom!
- Beeeep!
- Wheeee!
- Whooooo!
- Ouch!
- Yuck!
- Nom nom nom!
- Tap tap tap
- Tippy tippy tippy toes!
- Say whaaaat!
- okey dokey!
- Ni nah ni nah! (ambulance sound)
- Vroom vroom!
- (Any animal sounds)
- Bzzzz bzzzz
- Chugga chugga chugga

These sound effects are so important for non-speaking or minimally speaking children. They provide an easy sound bite for them to copy when ready. Even if they can't say words, you can recognize their attempt at a sound effect from the sound of their voice! Sound effects can act as a bridge on the journey from no words to words, as they can be highly motivating for your child to copy or try. They are also a more realistic goal than just expecting words out of nowhere.

Pick your soundbite or sound effect specifically to match the situation. Don't just throw lots of them in, all at once. It can be helpful to make a list of what your child likes to do right now and think about what kind of sound effects you could add, then write them down. Choose one or two sound effects per interest, so you get lots of opportunities to repeat those specific sound effects in a fun way when your child is enjoying those activities. Why do you think we want to keep them consistent? Because your child will have many opportunities to hear, enjoy, and even try to copy them!

As in an earlier example, if your child likes to poke things into the sand, you could start to poke it too and say 'poke poke poke!' as you do so, then pause. If your child likes the feel of the sand running through their fingers, you could join in and whisper '*Whoooshhhhhh*' as the sand runs through your fingers and their fingers, then pause. If you are playing with water, then '*Splishhhhh*' or *Splashhhhh*' are good sounds to make, then wait. When you open or close the curtain, add a '*Swishhhhhh!*' sound effect. When washing their feet, you could talk about their '*Tippy tippy tippy toes!*'. When tickling you could whisper '*Ticki ticki ticki!*'. Make sure you say your sound effect again while you do a fun thing like tickling their toes, then pause.

These soundbites can be unique to you and your child. You can make up your own ones and have fun with them. The sky's the limit! Get creative and silly, and see what happens when you bring more sound effects into your fun times together

'SOUND EFFECTS' VIDEO CHALLENGE

It's challenge time again! Record yourself with your child again for 2 or 3 minutes. Remember to follow all the previous strategies first. During your short play this time, you will focus on getting a good sound effect to fit the situation for whatever your child chooses to play or do. Try to keep it going with your child and find opportunities to bring that sound effect into the play for as long as your child is interested in that play. If they lose interest in the play and move on, get close and watch again to see if you can pick a new sound effect for the new interest. You can stop reading now and complete the challenge.

As you review your video, ask yourself if you managed to find a suitable sound effect.

1. Did your child stay interested so you could keep it going with the same sound effect?
2. Did you pause so your child could process what was happening or take a turn?
3. Did your child enjoy the sound effect and the silliness?
4. Did they respond in some way? How? And how did you respond?
5. How might you add some sound effects to your Short Repeatable Games?

You can note your thoughts here:

____

____

____

____

In this chapter you learned...

- what sound effects are
- sound effects are important to bridge the gap to mouth speech as they are easier for your child to potentially copy
- not to bombard your child with too many sound effects all at once but to choose relevant ones to what they are experiencing in the moment
- you can identify what your child is interested in most and make a list of some sound effects to match their interest that you can bring into play later as the occasions naturally arise

8

11 COMMON TRAPS

It's time to pat yourself on the back and consider how far you and your child have come since you began your journey using all these new strategies you have learned! Now you have had a taster of some of the most helpful tips to encourage authentic communication, it is time to look at some of the most common mistakes parents often make. You have already transformed many of your old ways and found new useful ways to interact with your child. But we must always remain vigilant as our old default ways are never too far away and could creep back in when we are not paying attention!

1. DON'T GIVE UP

Many parents may be strongly tempted to abandon using a strategy when they don't see immediate results. Be persistent! It can usually take 12 to 18 months for a child to learn to use language. For some, it takes longer. Just because you are not seeing your child use language doesn't mean that all your strategies are wasted. You are still helping your child develop their internal language for when they are ready to start using it, whether that be by mouth speech or by another method. Remember the 'pennies in the piggy bank' analogy? Whenever you use a strategy, it's like dropping a penny in. Over time they build up, and one day they might just overflow. Your child may need you to keep doing these strategies over a long period, even though you may not immediately see the benefit. But you may notice improvements in their interaction with you, and this needs to happen first to pave the way for progress in communication. These strategies are designed to be the shortest, most efficient way to help you help your child on their journey towards words, or if they are already using words, for them to use more words.

2. I MUST 'TEACH' LANGUAGE

This is the most common misgiving that gets in the way of authentic communication. Our goal is actually to foster as much joy as possible, not to 'teach' communication. As we mentioned before, we might teach a child independence skills, but communication is an entirely different kettle of fish. We can't 'teach' natural conversation by sitting down and doing 'work' or contriving a task. They have a 'work' radar, and they will know: If they detect that you are trying to teach communication, they will probably lose interest. Plus it won't be natural communication in real contexts, which we know is the best way for a child to learn to communicate. The best way to encourage natural language is to completely forget about 'teaching' and instead connect authentically with your child by having the most fun possible. Provide a language model for them without any expectation. Be your natural lovely self. You are more than enough! You can refresh your ideas on how to do this by revisiting Strategy 1: 'Get Out Of My Own Head' and Strategy 2: 'Get Involved and Have Fun!' and practise the video challenges again.

3. NOT RESPONDING TO MY CHILD'S VOCAL SOUNDS

Responding to your child's little sounds is such an important and impactful strategy! This is particularly relevant for children who typically communicate or ask for things physically. We have talked about how we get side-tracked by watching for visual signs of communication when they bring us something or lead us somewhere. We are primed to watch and interpret the physical signs indicating what they want.

Or we might get caught up on the 'doing' part of a game: how they complete the puzzle and put the shapes in the shape sorter. But while we are busy watching them doing these things, they might also be making little sounds that we may completely miss because we are hung up on watching or doing, and not listening.

It takes practice to remember to scan for the little sounds they might make while also thinking of how to respond in the moment so that we can acknowledge that we have heard them. You can go back to Strategy 3: 'Listen, REALLY Listen!' and Strategy 4: 'Respond with Enthusiasm' and complete the video challenges to practice these skills.

4. NOT PAUSING

One of the most common mistakes many parents make is to say lots of words or sentences back to back without pausing or not pausing for long enough. Remember how we talked about waiting 5-10 seconds after each of your comments? This is key for your child to process what has been said and to pair it with what has just happened so they can understand the meaning. If you load in more information and questions back to back, they won't have time to process your first comment. If this resonates with you, or if you know this is something you tend to do, this is your opportunity to go back and read Strategy 5, 'PAAAUUUSE'. Complete the challenges again to remind yourself of what pausing feels like.

5. TOO MANY QUESTIONS

This is a very common trap! We are primed as parents to test our children's knowledge by asking questions; we feel like this is the only sure way to check what they know. But what does it feel like for a child when we ask questions back to back? Imagine a friend of yours visiting you and firing question after question at you, barely waiting for you to answer each one. It would probably feel quite unpleasant! It likely feels similar for a child.

In addition, many minimally speaking children and Gestalt Language Processors may not understand the meaning of question words or understand the concept of questions. So they may seem to ignore them entirely, or may have learned how to respond to a particular type of question as a learned response ('What does the dog say?).

For all children, interesting comments, or statements, are most helpful for developing natural language because they are catchy 'earworms' for them to learn, internalize and potentially copy when they are ready, without the pressure of questions. You can revisit Strategy 4: 'Respond With Enthusiasm' to remind yourself of what you could say to your child and practice the video challenge again. Consider spending time on Strategies 1 and 2, move away from leading and practice picking up on what your child is interested in moment by moment instead, so you can add language to those things your child is thinking about.

6. SAYING TOO LITTLE

If you say too little, for example: if you focus on saying single words all the time, then your child may be drawn to naming lists of things. Your child won't get to hear how those words work as part of phrases and sentences. If your child starts to use single words or makes word attempts, this is an exciting time! Often, the natural reaction is to repeat the word they have just attempted. For example: if your child attempts to say '*Tiger!*', you might respond enthusiastically with '*Tiger!*'. This is okay if it is a once-off, but if this is your default, you may go back to Strategy 4, practise how to 'Respond With Enthusiasm' and complete the Video Challenge again. You should include a mix of different lengths in your chat: some sound effects, some single words and some phrases. Then you are covering the best of all worlds!

7. SAYING TOO MUCH

If your default is to say sentences that are longer than 5 or 6 words most of the time, you may pitch your language too high for your child to latch onto or understand. Depending on their expressive language level, it may not be achievable for your child to copy you. So when you include a mix of lengths: sound effects, single words and some 4-5 syllable phrases, this will ensure that you give your child the best possible chance to connect with what you are talking about, and you will be giving them enough fun sounding earworms to keep them hooked! Strategy 4: 'Respond With Enthusiasm' will help you think of the right things to say, and the video challenge will help you put it into practice.

8. TOO MANY IDEAS IN ONE PHRASE

Combining many ideas into one sentence can be great when your child is ready to build long, expressive sentences. But when your child is just starting their communication journey, it can confuse them. Try to focus on just one idea per sentence.

Several ideas are combined in this example: '*I like big black cats!*'. How could we alter it so there is only one idea per phrase? We could instead say: '*It's a cat!*'... '*It's so big!*'... '*It's black!*'... '*I like it!*'. Your child may be able to process what you say better if you break it down and say one idea at a time.

9. BORING OR REPETITIVE CHAT

We can all fall into this trap! We may run out of things to talk about and resort to narrating what a child is doing. For example, we may describe what they are doing with the 'blue truck' and the 'yellow car' over and over! But is this interesting to your child? It might be for a vehicle enthusiast who loves colors! But it may not be the most helpful strategy to build authentic communication.

Imagine you meet your friend for a coffee, and your friend tells you about a good movie they saw recently. The first time they tell you the plot, it's interesting, and you pay attention! But suppose your friend keeps talking about the same movie plot over and over again. In that case, it is no longer an authentic conversation, and you will soon lose interest. The same goes for your child: Although your child might enjoy listing things they know, it's much more fun to connect and talk about authentically interesting things. It can take practice to find interesting, new or intriguing things to talk about with your child. You can go back to Strategy 4: 'Respond With Enthusiasm', and practise finding fun sounds and comments to say that are of interest in the moment.

10. MISSING AN OPPORTUNITY FOR A SHORT REPEATABLE GAME

We all do this because we will naturally miss things when they happen live. When there is a lull in the play, we tend to take over again, lead or 'teach' to keep the interaction going. But the best spontaneous games emerge from the little moments when your child randomly tries something out and explores something in a new way. The lull in play might reveal a unique angle your child is exploring. They might use a toy 'incorrectly' or in a way that the toy was not intended for - putting a character down the car slide, putting a car into the doll's house, or throwing a soft teddy into a box. These are perfect opportunities to just go with and see where they lead! Notice these little moments and try to join in and repeat the interesting or intriguing experience over and over. When we do this, we may stumble across a short repeatable game that they will automatically enjoy because they chose it! Then we can add fun sound effects, words and short phrases that we can repeat again and again in a short space of time. This helps them to learn, remember, and even possibly copy them. You can revisit Strategy 1: 'Get Out Of My Own Head' to remember how to focus on your child's interests and notice these precious moments. You can also focus on Strategy 6: '10-20 Second Short Repeatable Games' to practise finding new games by doing the video challenge.

11. FINISH MY SENTENCE

Many parents are excited when their child attempts to say words! This is a wonderful time, and the temptation is to give many opportunities for a child to 'finish my sentence': For example, *'The cow says...?', 'It's a big red...?' 'Ready steady...?'*, and then waiting for them to fill in the last word. Some children may only use their words when someone else prompts language in this way.

This can be fun in the short term because it achieves immediate results: your child is using a word! But in the longer term, if you focus on these prompts to elicit language from your child, they will miss opportunities to experience authentic communication. How do we get around this? It is best to use comments or statements - just say the whole phrase and then wait! *'The cow says mooooo!', 'It's a big truck!' 'Ready steady GO!'*. Doing this shows your child how language works; they might join in WITH you, or volunteer a part of the phrase when they are ready, all by themselves.. Even if they don't, it's all adding pennies to the piggy bank, and one day it might overflow.

Your child will naturally focus on the last word you say. This allows your child to process and take in keywords from what you have said and link them to what they see happening at that moment, increasing their understanding of language. When you pause after your comment, you are also giving your child an opportunity to do or say something. Say your fun phrases with enthusiasm and show them what you are talking about by being animated and using big gestures. Your child may be more likely to want to join in and copy you! You can revisit Strategy 4: 'Respond with Enthusiasm' to revise what you could say instead of using prompted phrases. Try out the video challenge again.

9

WASH RINSE REPEAT

We have now covered all seven strategies to increase the number of opportunities for your child to communicate with you. We have also revised some common traps parents often fall into. You are fully equipped with a variety of tools in your communication strategy toolbelt!

If your child isn't quite using words, you may have noticed that they are engaging with you more or attempting to communicate more with you in other ways. They are progressing on their communication journey.

If your child is ready for words, you may have noticed them starting to copy you, initiating more interaction or communication with you and making more attempts at sounds or words. Keep it going! 'Wash Rinse Repeat', as long as it is fun for your child.

These strategies can never be used 100% perfectly because there is no such thing as a 'perfect interaction'. All we can do is look for opportunities we can work with at any given moment. Don't be discouraged when you look back at your videos and feel like you have forgotten everything you thought you knew and everything went 'wrong': There are no rights or wrongs. Remember that you are already naturally doing lots of great strategies all the time! But looking back allows you to notice the little things and spot new opportunities we often miss in the moment. The act of reflecting and practicing again and again will get you to the point where the parts you might find challenging will become second nature to you. Reflect each time on what happened and what you could do to implement a strategy even better next time. Whenever you create an opportunity for your child to do or say something, they might join in! And every time they choose to join in, they get a chance to practice some aspect of communication.

Plus, the single most important thing that will help move your child forward in terms of their ability to connect, interact and communicate with you is based on how much fun they are having. Our primary goal is to create as much joy for them as possible, and to create the circumstances for more connection if they are ready for that. If they are not having fun, abandon the activity. It's not working! And it's not likely to work if they are not intrigued, smiling, laughing and enjoying themselves.

Keep the momentum moving to keep your child engaged as long as possible, but if they lose interest and move on, move on with them. Do Strategy 1 again, 'Get Out Of My Own Head', and find something that interests or intrigues them or gets them giggling or laughing again. Then follow all the other steps you have learned in this book.

The quality of the interaction, not the quantity, will help your child make progress. If you are working and can only spend a short time with your child each day, that's okay! You don't have to feel like you or your child are missing out. You only really need to spend a few minutes at a time on your actual practice of these strategies.

This all makes sense on paper, and you may think that some of this book is stating the obvious, but we need to put this into active practice regularly over time and follow the plan to reap real benefits. Otherwise, you have just had a nice positive read with no outcome. And I guarantee you there is something we can all do more of! Just today I had a parent say to me that it all made sense in theory, but they missed their child's vocalisation attempts when they looked back on their video! By the end of their video coaching session, their child was enjoying making intentional sounds for the 'Crash' game, which only happened because the parent made a point of noticing and responding to their child's sounds.

The place where all the work happens is during the video challenges. Reflect on what you see, hear and practice, practice, practice so that much of this will become natural for you, then it won't be much effort at all. It will be something you do every time you interact with your child.

So I encourage you to revisit the challenges frequently to stay on track. Take charge of your own progress as the 'main therapist' for your child's communication. It can be so gratifying to realize your own potential and the power you possess to make a difference!

10

BONUS AREA

The following is an excerpt from the same author's upcoming book 'Supporting Early Communication Through Everyday Routines'. This new publication contains practical tips and suggestions for finding opportunities for your child to connect and communicate more with you during routines you already do every single day. It is meant to be read as an adjunct to this 'A Parent's Guide to Early Communication'. You are getting an exclusive sneak peek. Enjoy!

Building Strategies into Everyday Routines

We all have little ways that we do things each day. From the moment we get up in the morning to the moment we go to bed, we have a multitude of short routines like getting up, brushing our teeth, getting dressed, having breakfast, watering plants or even feeding family pets! These little daily repetitive routines and chores are ideal for helping our children to learn either of these two goals:

1. A ***'DOING'*** GOAL: Learning to physically do a part or parts of a specific routine.

2. A ***COMMUNICATION*** GOAL: Learning to communicate during a specific routine.

You need to be clear from the outset about which of these goals is best to focus on for your child, and this will depend on what they are already doing or communicating. We will cover this as we go through the book and apply the strategies.

How do we work these goals into routines? Well, it works like the 'Short Repeatable Games', but the repetition is daily instead of many times in the space of one minute. You may have a couple of chances to repeat a part of a routine in one minute: for example, in a dressing example, there are several opportunities for our 'doing' goal to put limbs 'in' something – two sleeves and two socks.

Let's go through some examples now and see what kind of goals apply best to different types of routines.

I'm Hungry!

Many young children stand by the refrigerator or the cupboard when they want something. Parents have to 'guess' what they want, but usually know their preferences!

Communication Goal: This situation lends itself more towards a communication goal. See what your child is already doing to let you know they want something. If your child is early in their communication journey, how do they communicate to you that they are hungry? Do they stand near what they want, make a sound, reach, or ask another way? Ideally, you want to say a phrase that includes their desired snack, like *'Let's get a drink!' 'Let's get a snack!' 'Let's get some grapes!'*. Then get the item you know they want and give it to them (*'Mmmm, yummy!'*) because they have already communicated what they want in the only way they know how. When you show them how easy it is to request in this way, they will want to do more of it and trust you as their communication partner. Of course, you still have to honor your parenting boundaries, so you will not give them their 5th cookie at bedtime! (See 'Yes/No' Strategies.)

Let's Have Some More!

This routine lends itself to a Communication goal: If your child wants more and it is okay to give some more, see how they ask you for more (Strategy 3). Remember to honor their first communication attempt. If they ask you in a new way or a way that is slightly further ahead, you can Respond with Enthusiasm! Remember to *Listen* - focus on how they communicate with you: by reaching, making sounds, and words.

Acknowledge - say 'Yes!' or 'okay!' with a nod and smile (or 'Later' / 'No' with a soft neutral expression). This will help them to feel validated and that this new way is useful.

Model and Show – say something they could say, 'Let's get some more!' 'Another one!', then *Give it right away* – they have already communicated to you what they want, so don't ask them to communicate or say it again.

Over time they will learn the power of their communication and want to experiment with communicating in new ways more, especially if you are an enthusiastic communication partner.

Getting My Bowl

Doing goal: if your child is not yet taking part in a routine, for example, breakfast, you can help them by handing them their bowl or spoon and showing them to the table. They will need a lot of help at first to do this. But eventually, they will come to know that they are to get their bowl or spoon themselves. If your child prefers to do their own thing and is not yet following either

11

CLOSING THOUGHTS

In the Introduction of this book, I voiced my hope for you to feel empowered and confident in trying out the strategies we have learned about. I hope to have met that goal. You now have the tools to start helping your child connect and interact more with you, and you won't go wrong as long as you and your child are having fun.

Remember that baby steps are definitely the way to go when trying to change how we do things. It is impossible to change and take on new ways of doing things overnight. You can also look for individual or group parent coaching. This kind of support could further help you to put some communication-enhancing strategies into practice.

Remember to seek professional advice if you have any concerns about your child's speech, language or communication development. Seek advice as soon as you notice your child is not making the progress you expect, so you can avoid pitfalls and get the right kind of advice and support. Waiting lists can be long, so don't delay in calling your local health advisor.

If you suspect your child is leaning towards a Gestalt way of learning or processing language, consider seeking a therapist familiar with working with Gestalt Language Processing.

If you have enjoyed reading this book, please consider leaving an honest review on Amazon to help other parents benefit from it. I wish you and your child connection and communication, but mostly a lot of fun together!

ALSO BY CAROLYN J. WEBB

Early Communication Pocketbook

3 Easy Steps to Enhance Your Child's Speech and Language Development in Just 7 Days!

Supporting Early Communication Through Everyday Routines

Effectively Target Speech, Language and Independence Skills in Toddlers With Easy Transformative Video Exercises

Promoting Early Communication In Play

Step-by-Step Parent Guide to Enhance Language in Toddlers and Preschoolers Through Everyday Fun Games With Transformative Video Exercises

Printed in Great Britain
by Amazon

39825275R00116